LOCKED UP
IN LA MESA

STEVE PETERSON & ELDON ASP

California, U.S.A.

The authors are grateful for the assistance of Roger Sachs, Ernesto Hernandez, Paula Peters, Roberto Salinas, Pawel Sasik and Bernardo Mendez.

Cover Photograph © 2011 by Darin Marshall

Printed in the United States of America

First Dirt City Press paperback edition, 2011

ISBN: 0-9837237-0-2
ISBN-13: 978-0-9837237-0-7

DEDICATION

STEVE PETERSON:

For every member of my huge, loving family.

ELDON ASP:

For Michelle (for everything)
and for Steve—thank you for sharing your
stories with me.

CONTENTS

Foreword

MY NAME IS STEVE PETERSON, and in 1974 I was sentenced to four and a half years inside of the worst prison in Mexico—which is saying something, because Mexican prisons in general are pretty ████████ bad.

It's gonna seem hard to believe at times, but everything in this book really happened, most of it exactly the way I describe it (although I have combined a few characters and events here and there to make it flow a little smoother). I've also included a couple small things that happened to friends of mine and I only heard about it—some stories are just too good to pass up. Lastly, I've changed a lot of the names. Even though it's nearly four decades later, there's a lot of good people who don't need their pasts dredged up, and a couple bad ones who might not appreciate me airing their dirty laundry.

In all other respects these stories are true, as crazy as they might sound. I lived through them, and after all this time I finally feel like I'm ready to share them with others. So imagine you just sat down on the next bar stool over, and I'll get started...

Burro

How It Went Down

THEY RECENTLY FILLED it in—I think it was Homeland Security that did it—but for years and years there used to be this little canyon running north/south through the mountains west of TJ. Everyone called it "Smugglers' Gulch." I guess they used to run all sorts of shit through there, but toward the end of the '60s on into the '70s, when the drug scene really got rolling, it was mostly pot. I mean *tons* of it, in big bales and tight little kilo bricks.

Guys would carry it over in backpacks, or on burros for the bigger loads. I think at that time a kilo was going for around forty bucks down in Mexico, and you could turn around and sell it for a couple hundred once you got it across the border. Good money, okay? And it was my feeling that it never should have been illegal in the first place, so when the

11

opportunity presented itself for me to make some quick cash smuggling pot I jumped at it, and that's how I ended up in the gulch that night.

The original plan, which I still think was pretty solid except for a couple key problems (mostly in the areas of tactics and personnel), was for me and my friend Chicago Joe to hike over the border from the American side, which was only a couple of miles, and then wait in the canyon while our other friend Roger drove up with the pot.

Shit, I gotta back up.

Before this, I had been in Colorado doing construction work at a little candy factory that my uncle owned out there. And back home where I was from, in Oceanside, California, this guy Roger, who I kind of knew because we moved in similar circles, was renting a room in my old house. One day I came home for a visit and Roger asked me if I wanted to get something going because he had heard I was a guy who could get things done. He'd heard I had a couple connections down in Mexico, and he had some guys back east in Tennessee or somewhere that wanted to get their hands on quite a bit of pot.

It was perfect timing for him to ask me because I really needed some cash, so right away I said yes. It didn't seem like that big a deal because in those days pot was everywhere and like I said, I knew it was illegal but I didn't believe that was right. (For some reason that seemed like a sensible thing to factor in at the time, the unfairness of the law. I look at it now and it's like, who gives a shit if it *should* have been illegal or not, it *was* illegal, and that should have been the end of the story right there. Well, whatever.) So I said, "Yeah, let me go down there and talk to some of my guys and we'll make it happen."

There were a few different connections down there that I could have called on, but most of them weren't right for one reason or another. For example, one of them, this dude Jorge, was a big player but just completely nuts. He lived in a big old hacienda and he had this .50-caliber machine gun mounted on a tripod up in the front window. He used to get wasted and shoot up the yard during parties just to freak everybody out—screw that. I had another guy, Joe (not Chicago Joe, a different one), down in Playas de Rosarito, and he had a regular house in town, although it had a wall around it, and there were broken bottles, all kinds of broken glass, stuck into the cement around the top to keep people from climbing over. I told him what I needed; he said he could get it no problem.

"When can you guys be ready?" he asked me. This was on a Wednesday, I believe, so I said we'd do it that weekend.

When I got back and told Roger the news he was so excited he could hardly stand it; we both were. We thought we were really doing something. We planned the whole thing out like a military operation—synchronized our watches, walkie talkies, the whole bit. It was pretty silly. The car we planned to use was a blue-green Chevy Vega station wagon with paisley curtains around the back and sides. (Believe it or not, that was a pretty inconspicuous car in those days.) Roger got it off his girlfriend, Barbara, who later on became his wife.

One thing I remember I was real proud of that was probably totally unnecessary but still pretty neat was this system I rigged up where you could pull a handle and open the hatchback without ever leaving the driver's seat. It was like a kind of rope-and-handle deal, attached to the latch. That was gonna save us valuable time, is what I figured. I'll explain that in a minute...

So Joe—Mexico Joe—had about a thousand kilos that he was prepared to sell us. We didn't have that kind of money available yet, so I told him we'd only take a little bit at first, and that I wanted to pay for the first load up front, sort of as a good-faith type of gesture. We had a little under five grand, enough for 120 kilos, so that's what we got. Our plan was we would smuggle that across the border, sell it, and then come back at a later date either with an inflatable raft, like a Zodiac, or else with a plane. Then we'd *really* be in business.

Joe had another place which was basically a shack with a trailer behind it, and that's where the pot was gonna be. On Friday we drove down—me and Chicago Joe in my truck, Roger, Barb and our other friend Mark Corey in the Vega. Those three went to a little motel in Rosarito and holed up there while me and Joe went to pack up the pot. We had four big army-style duffel bags that we'd brought with us. (They were nylon; this was around the time they were just coming out with the first nylon bags, which we chose because they were lighter than the canvas ones.) Anyway,

14

we went out back and unlocked the trailer and the smell just about floored us. Really good stuff, kilo bricks all wrapped up in crinkly green cellophane like you almost never see anymore. We loaded it up in the bags and got it all ready for the next day and then left it locked up in the trailer. After that we drove down to the motel and partied with the others, psyching ourselves up for the big mission we would do the next day.

When the time came, Joe and I drove back to the trailer and grabbed the bags of pot, then dropped them off with Roger and Barb at the motel. Then we had Mark drive us across the border in my truck. He dropped us off at the end of the gulch on the American side, which was basically farmland, real rural. This was around dusk; we wanted to get there when there was still a little bit of light so we could choose the best path through the rocks. The plan was for Mark to drive around for a bit and then come back and wait for us so he could pick us up when we came back with the pot. He was our getaway driver.

We crossed south through the gulch no problem. It was mostly deserted, just a couple small families and some young dudes by themselves, all sneaking north. We were the only ones heading south, because who the hell sneaks *into* Mexico? Anyway, we knew we were getting close to the end when we could hear the sounds of the traffic coming from the highway up ahead. I got down on my belly in the bushes and watched the road. Joe hung back in the canyon. Everything looked good, so I switched on the walkie talkie and pressed the button to send Roger the signal (there was a button you could press, for Morse code or whatever). After a few seconds his signal came back. All right, here we go.

I watched the road, and pretty soon I saw his headlights. I sort of waved at Joe hiding back there in the rocks, to let him know to get ready. And I watched real carefully as Roger drove past on the far side of the road. I didn't see anyone following him so I gave him the signal again. (There was a little overpass down the road a bit, and the plan was for him to cross the highway and come back to the pullout where Joe and I were waiting once I gave him the all-clear.)

So Roger crossed the overpass and eased the Vega off the highway right in front of us. This is where my rope contraption came in—he flapped open the hatchback right from the driver's seat as we ran out of our hiding places. The duffel bags had handles on the ends of them, and Joe and I grabbed hold of two each while Roger hit the gas. All told, he was stopped at the pullout for no more than about two or three seconds. As the bags slid off the back, I looked over at Joe, and I saw that he was looking at the road. He looked real scared, so I turned to see what had him so spooked. Directly in front of us, on the other side of the highway across the little grass median, a Tijuana city cop car went past, and these guys were *hauling ass*. I didn't see them slow down or look at us, not at all, so I figured we were probably okay, but when I turned back to Joe he was already gone. He left the bags right where they landed and just booked back up the canyon. I couldn't believe how fast he ran. Roger and Barb were gone too, just like we planned. I was all by myself with four huge bags of pot.

The first thing I did was drag two of the bags—*Joe's* two bags, I thought, all bitter—over to the bushes and stash them there, kind of covering them up with some brush. Then as I was heading back to grab the other two, I got a funny feeling like I'd better check for the cops. I figured there was no way in hell they had seen us, not when they were going that fast, but I had to be sure, so I kind of crept out to the edge of the pavement and looked down to where the overpass connected with the near side of the highway, where they'd be coming from if they were coming for me. I didn't see them, but my sight line was obstructed by a little outcropping of rock that clipped the corner of my view, so I couldn't actually get a clear look all the way to the ramp.

But anyway, I figured I was in the clear, so I went to grab the other two bags. I decided to stash one and carry the other, because there were several stretches of the canyon where you had to hoist the stuff up from one ledge to another; this was definitely a two-man job. I figured I could probably swing it if I only had to wrestle one bag up to the next ledge, but two would be pushing it. All of this was running through my head as I dragged those bags around... then I heard the crunch of car tires on gravel, fifteen or twenty yards off. I ran over and poked my head out, saw the cop car creeping up with its lights off. That's how they snuck up on me, they just cut the lights and cruised right up to the pullout. Needless to say, I dropped the pot and bolted.

I was wearing cowboy boots, which turned out to be a poor choice because they skidded and slipped all over in the loose rock, but I booked up the canyon, back up Smuggler's Gulch, and in no time at all I heard the cops behind me, already closing in on me and yelling at me to stop. And then they started shooting. That was the first time anybody had ever intentionally fired a gun at me, that I was aware of. I near about shit my pants; I'm serious. So I poured it on, but the next shot was even closer. It went right past my head and exploded against the canyon wall. There was shrapnel from the rocks, little chips of it, flying back at me, it was so close. And that was it—I wasn't taking any more chances.

My heart was just pounding, but I stopped where I was and I put my hands up high as I could and I turned around and marched back out of the gulch toward these cops. The whole time, I was yelling "¡Cálmate!" over and over, which means "chill out," basically. ██████ "Don't kill me," right? And these guys were yelling back at me and I had no idea what they were saying, but their attitude was really frantic. I don't know if they thought it was a trick, like Joe was gonna shoot them from up in the rocks someplace, but just as I was thinking it was over, like the whole situation oughta be winding down because I just gave up, these guys were getting more and more agitated. I wished I spoke better Spanish so I could know what the hell they were saying, if they were telling me to do something, so I could do it, because even though I was trying to surrender, I was starting to think they might shoot me anyway. I admit, part of me

18

was thinking "Shit—I should have kept on running."

I got almost all the way over to them and they still hadn't shot me, so that was good. They were still yelling, but at least they could tell I was unarmed and they could see that I was just completely freaked out. So I didn't look like a guy who was pulling a fast one. Still, they weren't taking any chances with me. As soon as I got close enough, the first guy took his pistol butt and clocked me with it, right behind the ear, and I went down. They jumped on me and cuffed me and beat me up some. Then they lifted me up to my feet and started marching me out of there, back toward the car. And I know I'm screwed for the two bags sitting right out in plain sight, but they still hadn't found the rest of the pot, so at that point I was actually thinking we might be able to salvage something out of the situation.

No such luck, because they had these flashlights, these shitty weak little flashlights, and they were shining them on the trail as we walked out of there, and one of them for some reason just swept his flashlight over at the last second and spotted a corner of one of the bags. That's it, it was over; I was twice as screwed. They smacked me around some more and shoved me in the car and then they went back for the bags. I was looking out the back window and I could see them tossing those bags in the trunk: Whump! Whump! Whump! Whump!

In Mexico the drug laws are actually fairly harsh; that was enough pot to ruin my life, and I knew it. So I was bumming out pretty hard on the ride back into town, as you can imagine. These guys were laughing at me and talking to me in Spanish so I didn't have any idea what they were saying, except when one of them said, *"Tienes dinero?"* Do you have any money?

Well shit—of course! This was Mexico! *Of course* I should have brought some money for bribes, but I didn't even think of it. What I should have done is bought about a hundred kilos of pot off of Mexico Joe, or even a little less maybe, and then saved the rest of the cash for an emergency just like this one. Because I swear to God, for five hundred bucks they would have definitely let me go. For a thousand they would have let me keep the pot, and for two thousand they might have even helped me get it across the border. We didn't think of that in our big master plan.

So I was sitting there kicking myself, feeling about as low as it gets, and by now we were all the way back in town, driving along through the busy streets. All of a sudden the cop in the shotgun seat started getting real agitated; he was talking fast and pointing at something a few cars up in the next lane over. The other guy kind of craned his neck to try to see it, and I started doing the same and then I was just like, "You gotta be kidding me." It was Roger and Barb in the Vega. Remember, their one job after pulling over with the pot and popping the hatchback and all that was they were supposed to turn around and head back to the motel and lay low. So what were they doing hanging around TJ? I don't know if they stopped off for a drink, or if they got spooked and figured maybe they would head for the border right then or what, but here they were, and that cop recognized them. He recognized the car, I should say, so maybe it wasn't as inconspicuous as we thought.

I don't think they even had a siren in there, or at least it wasn't working if there was one. The one cop, the driver, just kept on honking the horn while the other guy leaned out the window and waved his arms around, trying to get over. Finally he stuck his gun out the window and waved that around, and that worked; people let him in. So we got behind Roger and he pulled over to the side. He really didn't have any other choice because there was so much traffic. There was nowhere for him to go.

The cops jumped out and ran over to the Vega. They hauled Roger and Barbara out, pretty roughly, and cuffed them and threw them in the back with me. We got going again, just driving around in big circles because the cops were gonna try to shake those two down now, to see if they had any money. So we were all in the back there, and of course we had to pretend that they got the wrong people, like it was all some big misunderstanding, so we couldn't let on that we knew each other. We were whispering back there, and I was like, "Dude, what the fuck?!" They just shrugged and shook their heads or whatever, trying to explain it without really saying anything. Then the cops started in with the money talk.

I don't think Barb spoke much Spanish if any, but Roger had a fair bit; more than me, anyway. I was catching maybe every tenth word, but he had a pretty good idea what they were asking him, and he just sat there shaking his head. No dinero, no way. That was basically his position. Which is bullshit, because he could have gotten his hands on some emergency cash if he really wanted to. His connection, the bigwig in Tennessee— Greg was his name, or maybe Craig—he could have wired some money to a bank or whatever, and these guys would have been okay with that. They didn't give a shit, they just wanted some money. The way it works, what they would have done is they would have dropped Roger off somewhere close to the border, then hauled me and Barb in and booked us on a lesser charge, something they could easily make go away once Roger got his hands on the money. Either that or they could take us and hide us someplace, like a private home for example. They'd hold us hostage, is really what it amounted to, until Roger came through with the ransom.

So I was back there next to him and I was trying to say, "Roger, give 'em some damn money," you know, and he said,

"There is no money, Steve."

I don't know if he was just scared or what, or if maybe he thought it would make him look guilty if he came up with a bribe, but he had some reason. He just dug in his heels and he wouldn't budge.

"There is no money, Steve."

The cops couldn't believe it. Here they had these three white Americans, and we're on our way to a Mexican prison, which is like everybody's worst nightmare, and we can't even come up with a few hundred bucks to save our skins; it didn't make any sense. Shaking bribes out of scared gringos was half the job for these guys. And they had some kind of sixth sense for it, I swear. I don't think they had a radio in the car, so I don't know how anyone else found out about us, but I looked out the back at one point and there were two more cruisers following us, and then I looked again later and there were four, like they knew these guys had some big fish on the hook. Anyway, obviously, with every new cop that tagged along, the price was going up. If we were gonna buy our way out now, we were gonna have to come up with a whole shitload of money. But still Roger swore there was nothing, so it didn't matter, I guess. Our fate was sealed.

Steven L. Peterson y Roger Carl Sachs, detenidos por la Policía Municipal en posesión de 120 kilos de mariguana.

They screwed up the order of the names in the caption, but from left to right, that's "Barbara," Roger and me the night they arrested us. I look like a baby.

Candado

La Ocho

THEY TOOK US TO THE Eighth Street Jail, the one they called "*La Ocho*." There were a bunch more cop cars out front when we got there and also some news reporters and local politicians—those kind of people, important people in the community. I guess word had got out somehow that these guys were bringing in some pretty serious *traficantes*. Dangerous criminals. So everybody wanted to know about it or be associated with the bust in some way.

So we got there and they marched us into the place, and the first thing they did was drag us up some stairs to this little room, just a little cinder block room, and they stood us up in front of this table. On top of the table they had all these kilos piled up, and I knew it wasn't the same pot, for two reasons: A) they

25

didn't have time to get all our pot from the car to the room and stack it up all neat like that; and B) there was too much of it, way too much. It was total bullshit—just a fake photo-op setup.

So they stood us there and took a bunch of pictures—of us, of us in front of this pile of pot, of the pot by itself—and then they took us back downstairs and threw us in separate holding cells, me and Roger in a men's cell and Barb next door in the women's. Hers wasn't nearly as crowded as ours, but she definitely had it worse. That first night was just terrible. The guards and trusties kept coming around to get a look at the white girl, all whistling and talking dirty (you could tell even if you didn't know Spanish). At one point they strip-searched her and then later on one of the trusties unzipped his fly and pissed into the cell by her feet. They all laughed at that. She was barely keeping it together.

Over in our cell, Roger wasn't doing too great either. He'd never been in any kind of jail before, and he was pretty scared. I told him, I said,

"Roger, whatever happens in here you gotta promise me you ain't gonna cry, all right?" I told him whatever happened we could probably handle it as long as he didn't start crying. I had had a little bit of experience with jail (nothing major), so I wasn't quite as shocked as he was, but this *was* pretty awful.

The cell was maybe six feet wide by about eight feet deep. There were two sets of bunk beds, one on each side, and at the back of the cell there was a hole in the floor—that was the toilet. It was a four-man cell; I counted 21 prisoners in there when we showed up, making it 23 total. We got in so late that almost everybody else was already sleeping. There were three guys on each bunk, and the rest of 'em were packed on the floor like sardines in a can. We had to stand up the whole first night, that's how crowded it was.

First thing the next morning, we started trying to weasel our way into a better spot in the cell. I tried to put on this attitude, not real aggressive, but definitely sure of myself and, you know, not somebody you'd want to fuck with. I told Roger to kind of follow my lead. There was one rack of bunk beds right next to us, with three guys up on the top bunk, and at one point in the morning the biggest dude up there climbed down and went to the back of the cell to take a leak. And I didn't say anything, I just hauled myself right up there in his spot and gave the other two guys the dickeye. As soon as one of them jumped down Roger climbed up there with me and then we had the last guy outnumbered and he climbed down too. After that we held that bunk every moment for the next seven days. When one of us had to piss, the other one would stretch out and block the bunk from anyone climbing up; that's how we held the high ground.

It wasn't as hard as I'm making it sound. The other prisoners were way more messed-up than we were, almost without exception. I'm talking about drunks, junkies, country kids who were practically starving to death they were so malnourished, and just these total derelicts from the worst parts of TJ. It was a sad collection of individuals. Jesus Christ. They were all Mexican as far as I could tell, except for this one old Rastafarian-looking guy with long gray dreadlocks. He was from Belize, I believe; he was the worst.

The Rasta was always smiling—in that place! That was the first sign that he was mentally nuts. I'm not sure he'd even committed a crime; my hunch is the cops just had nowhere else to put him. He was a horrible sight, depressing, and absolutely crazy. It was the kind of crazy that starts to feel contagious after a couple of days. Someone said he'd been locked up in that tiny cell for five months already before we showed up; where his mind went all that time I have no idea. One image I don't think I'll ever shake is him taking a leak, and the whole time he's pissing, he's dancing around with these mincing little steps—like tiptoe-through-the-tulips kind of steps—and literally *bathing* with his own urine, scooping it up with his hands and splashing it all over his face, all over his hair. That was about the worst thing I'd seen in my life up to that point. I guess I've seen worse since.

Anyway, the food was as bad as the rest of it. Once a day, they'd wheel this big iron pot around on a cart, and everybody would gather around. They'd give you one tortilla apiece— stale, of course—and then they'd scoop out this ladle full of watery beans and just plop them right onto the tortilla, boiling hot. So you'd be standing there, and it would be burning the shit out of your hands, and you'd have to try to blow on it to cool it off or whatever, and at the same time try not spill it

28

because that was all you got for the day. It was ridiculous. After a few days, someone came to visit us, I forget who it was, but we sent him out to bring back tacos, and this guy came back with real tacos for everybody in the cell. That was a highlight. It worked, too, because nobody tried to get the top bunk from us after that.

Overall, though, the situation was still just impossible, especially for Roger and Barb. She was crying pretty much constantly now, and I could tell Roger was starting to lose it, too; he was praying all the time and he didn't look right. He said our getting busted was a sign from God telling us to clean up our act. I told him it was a sign that we needed a better plan, so I drew one up right there. It was pretty elaborate, with a Zodiac and wetsuits and fishing gear and all sorts of stuff going on. I did it mostly to distract Roger and try to lift his spirits. It didn't work, though. He and Barb were in awful shape; we had to do something. Lucky for them (unluckily for me), something occurred around this time that gave me an idea.

As the week went on, some guys were transferred out, some they let go, and some new ones were brought in. And one night they brought in this group of U.S. Marines—I think there were maybe six or seven of them—and they'd fucked up bad on their furlough down in TJ. They decided they were gonna bring a little pot back to their base, which was Camp Pendleton just north of San Diego. They went the beach route (where I wanted to go when we got our hands on a Zodiac) and got picked up by the federales while they were sneaking around the fence. I don't know exactly how much they had, but it was a tiny quantity, just enough to say they'd done it, really. They were probably fairly drunk; I think that's safe to say. And now they were scared.

One of them, this big handsome farm boy type named Hank, seemed a little more composed than the others. He was looking around, obviously thinking there was no way in hell his buddies could make it, not like he could. So he called the guards over and swore to them that he'd acted alone, that the pot was his and the others didn't know anything about it. He kept saying it louder and louder until eventually they let him sign a declaration—a confession, basically—that put the whole rap on him and let his buddies off the hook. The second he signed, they let the other guys go; the kid was a hero! Well, that was the answer right there.

The federales had a weak case at best against Roger and Barb. They weren't caught with anything, and they hadn't admitted any crime. I, on the other hand, was fucked. So to save everybody the hassle and expense of a crooked show trial, I signed a declaration that said I'd never seen the other two before in my life, that it had been me alone with the pot, and my friends went free. (The next day I signed a second declaration swearing that the guards beat me with hoses to make me sign the first one. I figured it couldn't hurt to try, and even the guards seemed to get a kick out of that.)

Before they left, with Barb bawling her eyes out and thanking me over and over, I took Roger aside and I made him promise me that he was gonna do everything in his power to get me out, whatever he could do from the outside to help me.

Now I was all alone, and I have to say I felt a little better for it. I knew I could handle whatever the situation could throw at me. Not easily, of course, not happily, but I could take it. With Roger and Barb safe on the outside, I could quit worrying about them and focus on my own survival.

The biggest threat to that, next to the awful conditions, was probably the guards. They were like mean animals, like when a cat gets ahold of an injured bird. They got off on the control they had over the guys inside, and they were obsessed with getting confessions, which, since I'd already signed mine voluntarily, they didn't need to wring out of me. That was an unexpected benefit; there was no longer any need to interrogate me. Other guys, the ones who still swore they were innocent, were basically tortured, almost every day. The guards took them to a windowless concrete box where they beat them with hoses or other tools. Sometimes they'd put tape over the guy's mouth and then shake up a can of soda and open it right under his nose so the carbonation would burn and fizz in his sinus cavities. The guys who'd been through it said it hurt worse than the beatings. There was never any problem getting confessions out of people; the rate was close to a hundred percent, eventually.

But sometimes even that wasn't exciting enough for the guards. When they got really bored, they'd hold fights in the hallway outside the cells. Just like in any prison, there were all sorts of enemies locked up, guys from different gangs or just guys who had a beef with each other on the outside for whatever reason. There was always a lot of trash-talking back and forth between the cells. So once in awhile the guards would let two enemies out into the corridor and it was just like a human cockfight. They'd go at each other with all that hate and anger boiling up in them from the situation they were in. Two guys who'd maybe had a minor argument about a girl or a little bit of money would become mortal enemies. There was betting just like a cockfight, too, and the guards loved it. They'd laugh and cheer, and then when they'd had enough, one of them would get a hose and spray the fighters until they broke it up, just like you'd do with a couple of dogs humping in your yard. I remember one fight between a young kid in my cell and an older, bigger guy from down the hall somewhere. I don't know what it was about, but they went at it and the kid got the worst of it, by far. After they broke it up, he came back to the cell and his nose was smashed sideways on his face, just totally flattened, and of course he didn't get any kind of medical attention; of course not.

What else? The trusties. They were pretty much as bad as the guards. They were long-term inmates who were basically really good at kissing ass. Nobody liked them, but they sucked up so much that they were rewarded with jobs in the jail and more freedom than the rest of us. And what they used that freedom for mostly was thieving. They'd steal anything they could get their hands on, and if they couldn't get their hands on it they had other tricks.

I remember watching one night just fascinated as one old prick literally *fished* a wallet from a guy's pocket while he slept on the top bunk inside the cell. The trusty's job was to mop the hallway outside of the cells, and he came back with his mop after lights-out. He had part of a wire coat hanger jammed into the end of the mop handle so that the hook was hanging down, and what he did was he sort of gently poked this guy until he rolled over in his sleep. The first few times the guy didn't move enough, so the trusty would wait a few minutes and then give him another tiny poke with the hook, just enough to make him roll around a bit to find a more comfortable spot. When he got him where he wanted him, he worked the hook into the guy's pocket until he snagged the wallet, and then he held his breath and reeled it back out through the bars. The whole process took at least forty-five minutes, I'm sure. The patience and skill involved was simply unreal. I saw the trusties steal all sorts of things that way: wallets, clothes, leather belts, shoes—anything that could be converted to cash. I had a brand-new Levi's jacket which Roger had given me before he left, and even though it was about a size and a half too small, I made sure to keep it on and buttoned up at all times after I'd seen what they were capable of.

I only spent probably three or four days on my own in La Ocho after Roger and Barb got out, but it was really starting to wear me down, the boredom and the crowding and the stench worst of all. I was only twenty-five years old, but lying in the same cramped position on that hard concrete bunk was turning me into an old man. Finally on the eleventh day after my arrest, word came down the prison grapevine that the federales had arrived to take some of us to the pen: *Penitenciaría de La Mesa.*

I had heard stories about La Mesa, the notorious state prison on the east side of town. Those who'd survived it made it sound like an absolute nightmare, with one important exception: in La Mesa, you could move around freely, indoors and out. After almost two weeks in La Ocho, I would have gladly risked anything just for a chance to breathe fresh air and to see the sky again. I couldn't wait to go.

When they called my name, I worked my aching body down off that bunk for the last time. Two guards came up to the cell with a couple of federales. They unlocked the door and waved me over. I hobbled out, and one of the feds grabbed me hard and slammed me up against the bars. I resisted, naturally, and his buddy cracked me in the head with his pistol butt. Then they cuffed me and hauled me out of that dark humid hole to the street outside. I felt like I was gonna go blind in the sunlight, it was so bright, but I loved it. I took huge deep breaths of that shitty Tijuana air, just filling my lungs. God, it felt good to be outside.

It didn't last, of course. They threw me in the back of an old police van with several others and drove us across town to the headquarters of the federal police. Once there, they lined us up and marched us to a holding cell in the back of the building. At the cell door, one by one, they took off our handcuffs and shoved us inside, a lot harder than they had to. One of the federales was the same fat-faced bastard who'd pistol-whipped me back at La Ocho. He pushed me around until I mouthed off and then he pulled his gun and wound up to hit me again. This time before he could clock me I threw up my forearm to block him. I saved my head but I came away with a knot the size of an egg just below my elbow. His buddies all laughed, but I think it was as much at him as at me; they didn't seem to like him any more than I did.

Anyhow, with that little bit of excitement out of the way, the cops moved on and I checked out the new cell. The other prisoners were all sitting on this low bench that ran around the perimeter. There were no bunks; it was more like a waiting room, but with bars. It was dark in there, and I noticed there were tiny specks of dust caught in a skinny little shaft of sunlight. I followed it with my eyes up to a tiny hole in the plaster of the ceiling. Beyond that was the open sky.

The border couldn't have been more than a mile or two away. If I could make it, I'd be home free. There was no way anyone would bother chasing me once I was back in the States, and no way they'd bother extraditing me on such a pissant little case. There were definitely risks: the other prisoners could rat me out to the federales, or I could get my head blown off as soon as I popped up out of the hole; still, I had to try it. I at least had to try it. The sun would be going down soon; there was no better time to make my escape.

The hole was in the corner, and I found I could reach it without much trouble if I stood on the bench below. The plaster was dry, and harder than it looked, but with some scratching and scraping and pulling I was able to loosen a few pebble-size chunks and crumble them off. One of the guys who'd come over in the same van from La Ocho climbed up to help me. I guess he wanted out as bad as I did. At first the others just stared at the floor, or shook their heads like we were crazy, but when they saw it was working they got into it. There wasn't room on the benches for more than two guys to work at a time, but they kept a lookout for us and kicked the loose chunks out of sight so it wouldn't be too obvious what we were up to.

We'd gotten the hole open about a foot in diameter—almost there!—when somebody whispered that the feds were coming, so we all scattered and sat down real fast. The door opened and in walked the same fed, Pudgy, the one who'd roughed me up. He did a slow lap of the cell, eyeballing everybody, and even stopped right under the hole at one point, but he never looked up. I was the only white guy in there, the only American, which I guess made me some sort of candidate for special treatment, because he made his way over to me and stood right in front of me. It's weird the things you remember, but I can still picture the sweat running down his face, hanging on the end of his nose until it finally dripped off. He looked at me for a while, real mean, and then made some kind of grunting sound and kicked his leg at me, but I dodged it. Then he pulled me to my feet and shoved me out the door. On my way out I gave a little nod to the guy who'd helped me with the hole, like, "Good luck, partner."

Pudgy and this other fed took me outside and around the building to a wooden staircase that went up to a little office. I remember the office was painted three different shades of blue, with red and yellow trim. There was a ceiling fan in the middle of the room, all wobbly and rusty but it worked. There were three secretaries at wooden desks spread out around the room. Two were these kind of heavy older ladies, and they were having some deep conversation with each other about something. They never even looked up. The third one was younger, maybe late thirties, and really attractive. Her desk was right next to a window, and that's where they told me to go sit down. She didn't look up either at first, just kept on typing, so I sat across from her and looked out the window and also peeked at her breasts a little bit, I'll admit. Finally she looked up at me and smiled.

"Hello," she said. It was the first time someone had treated me with anything like basic human kindness in nearly two weeks. I smiled back and said hello. She asked if I spoke Spanish. I said no. Still smiling, she got up and went over to talk to the federales, Pudgy and the other guy. I guess they were figuring out what to do with me. They looked over at me a few times, and when they saw I was watching, they slipped outside so they could talk on the stairs without me seeing them. The other two ladies kept their heads down, chatting; they paid no attention to me.

I was all alone next to an open window. Holy shit.

My palms were all sweaty and my heart was beating so fast I felt sick. I could see the ground outside, and I imagined how I'd land and roll and sprint away down the alley. I could also easily imagine them waiting for me outside, so instead of jumping down and escaping I'd jump down and get shot dead. It was either my last chance at freedom, or a trap. Stuck between the two possibilities, I just sat there paralyzed until the door opened and my window closed, so to speak. It was a relief, to be honest. I wanted out, but not like that; the risk was too scary. The pretty secretary sat back down and finished her typing. Then she waved Pudgy over and he cuffed my hands and herded me back down the stairs and into the van again.

The inside of the van was just a plain metal box and it was boiling hot. No benches or windows. It smelled like years of old vomit. There were about six or seven of us altogether, I believe, with our hands cuffed behind our backs. I wasn't sure of the exact number because who cares and also because it was pitch black with the doors closed. They basically threw us in there like we were sides of beef, or garbage bags; they didn't care.

So we got rolling, and after about a block or two I figured out what the puke smell was all about. There were no shocks or springs or anything, is what it felt like, and it seemed like they were hitting every pothole on purpose. So in the back there we were bouncing all over the place and sliding side to side around the corners and banging into each other in the total darkness. Remember, half these guys were junkies in full-on withdrawal from something or other, so they were pretty much ready to throw up just walking around. How we avoided getting puked on on that trip was some kind of miracle. It wasn't a very long drive, I guess that was it.

Anyway, so we bumped along for a while and then we stopped and after a couple minutes they threw the doors open and dragged us out. And there it was, right in front of me: La Mesa. The sun was pretty much down now but I could see the walls sort of looming over me, beige walls, wider at the top so the guards could walk around on them. Gun towers every hundred feet or so. And looking up at it, the whole truth of the situation just *landed* on me. I was trying to keep it together but inside I was like, "Holy shit," you know?

"What have I gotten myself into?"

.

Sopilote

Okay, Showtime

THE FEDERALES SHOVED ME AND the other new guys into this chain-link cage attached to the front of the prison, sort of like an entryway or a sally port, and that's where they planned to process us before they threw us to the wolves inside.

I call 'em wolves, but they were really more like vultures. I could see them through the fence and Jesus, they looked terrible. Filthy, like villains straight out of a John Wayne movie. Twitchy, evil-looking, eyes just dead, like snakes or something. They were all pressed up against the fence and looking us over. I don't remember anyone licking their lips, but they might as well have; it was that kind of a look. Just up and down, up and down, checking us out, checking out our stuff, like they were window shopping. It was freaky.

I knew the only way I'd survive was if I kept my cool. Be cool, and stay cool. I wouldn't be a dick to anybody, I wouldn't act like a tough guy, but I wouldn't be a victim either. Even though I felt like I wanted to puke and cry and run away just looking at those guys on the other side, I played it cool.

Then the *comandante*—the warden—came out to give us a little speech. It was in Spanish, so most of it went right over my head, but whatever—I doubt it would have helped me much even if I had understood it. He was this little nerdy guy, not very impressive, but he seemed decent enough. He had a few buddies with him, and one of them I just took an immediate dislike to right off the bat: this big fat piggy-looking guy with tiny eyes. Real mean eyes.

The warden finished his talk and this piggy dude stepped forward, digging in his pockets like he was looking for change. The vultures started getting real animated all of a sudden, agitated. They crowded around on their side of the fence like they knew what was coming. So the guy pulled his hand out and it *was* change, he had a handful of change, and he tossed it through the fence like he was scattering seed. You know that move? And the whole time, he was laughing this real mean laugh. The vultures on the other side, man, you would have thought it was diamonds this guy threw. They pounced on those coins like they would kill each other for them. Punching, kicking, wrestling—and these are just nickels, basically. Small change.

So this fat dude and his buddies, the warden and everybody, they were laughing away like they were having a great old time, and it was just gross. But I looked at those poor junkies—I mean, I knew they'd slit my throat in a second if I let them, so I don't mean I thought they were nice guys or anything—but I looked at them and I felt bad for them. I was thinking, "Jesus Christ, look at these guys! Where's their friggin' pride?" You know what I mean? Like, how do you let yourself get to the point where you're gonna fight a guy halfway to the death for a damn nickel? And then it hit me. I remember thinking in the moment: "Oh shit—what if that's me?" Like, what if I was looking at a vision of my own future? Because I bet those guys didn't start out that way, either. That was a depressing thought.

Then the warden and his pals, the pig-looking guy, they all cleared out of there and then they opened up the gates and shoved us inside. "Oh, boy," I thought, "here we go." My hands were shaking but I stuck them in my pockets and strolled in there like I was taking a walk on the beach. That's the look I was going for, anyway.

The way those vultures swarmed us, it was like *we* were the coins. Most of the guys I was with, the new guys, were small and weak or sick or strung-out or obviously scared or whatever; they were easy targets. So for most of them, anything they had that was worth stealing was gone pretty much right away. Some of them just gave it up without a fight, and the rest got their ass kicked and then gave it up. A few of the new guys were obviously veterans of the place, or places like it. You could tell they weren't guys to fuck around with. They walked in like they owned the place and nobody bothered them at all, or they said hi to them, welcomed them like they were guests showing up at a party. The guys sort of in the middle, like me, the ones who didn't look like badasses but didn't really look like pushovers either, we got surrounded, and there were basically two choices: either fight it out right there with the whole crowd and definitely lose, or kind of go with the flow and bide our time, try to find some better odds down the line a little bit and make our stand then.

So I went strolling in there, and of course I stuck out like a white crow. Here I am, I'm this young surfer kid from California with my blue eyes and my curly blond hair. "*Borrego*," they called me, which means lamb. (I found out much later that, as a nickname, it also means "dummy." Bastards.) So right away I was surrounded, and it was kind of like being at a concert or something, when you're in a big crowd and it just carries you along wherever it wants to go. These guys all circled around me, checking me out, tugging at my jacket, patting me down, looking for my wallet. I just tried to shrug them off and keep walking, but the crowd kept pushing, and I went where they went.

After maybe a dozen yards or so I looked around and realized that I couldn't see any of the other new guys I'd come in with, like maybe they'd separated us, on purpose or not I didn't know. There was a pretty sizeable crowd around me, and I saw that they were moving me toward this big fenced-in area, sort of a compound within a compound. (I found out later it was called the "*corral*.") Beyond the chain link fence were several structures that looked like concrete bunkers, painted bright blue. I got a real bad feeling when the crowd herded me inside of that cage, and when we started heading for one of those buildings, I about lost it.

Not that there was anything I could really do about it. The thing about playing it cool is, as soon as you stop, everyone knows you were just playing; you can't go back again. You gotta pick your moment, and you better make it count. I wanted to be sure the situation was as bad as it was gonna get before I freaked out and let everyone see how scared I really was. Out there in the open, it's not like there were any guards around or anyone who'd give a shit if I got my ass kicked or even if I got stabbed, so I wasn't any safer making my stand out there than I would be inside that bunker. At least inside I might be able to get my back against the wall so they couldn't get me surrounded.

That was my plan, anyway, as they pushed me through the door and into the darkness—I'd wait as long as I could and then try to get my back against the wall and just go so apeshit on them that the rest would think twice about stepping up to try me. There was basically no chance of a plan like that actually working, of course, but the two alternatives I saw—just handing my shit over, or picking a fight with the whole crowd when they had me surrounded—were even worse. And I wasn't thinking completely clearly, as you can probably imagine.

So in we went, into the big blue concrete box, (or "tank," they called it). Inside it was dark and it took a minute for my eyes to adjust, but when they did, it was actually kind of incredible: it looked like an indoor shantytown, with little apartments (called "*carracas*") stacked like rickety tree houses two or three high all the way up to the ceiling. And I mean *really* rickety: the inmates built them themselves out of old wood, cardboard—literally cardboard—anything they could get their hands on. They were all painted in various bright colors. It was quite a sight. And running right down the middle the full length of the place, there was a long wooden picnic bench, a continuous picnic bench about thirty yards long, and that also had a real festive paint job.

As I took this all in, they pushed me further and further into the place, toward one room in particular. (About halfway down on the left side, I believe it was.) As they were doing this, a new plan sort of sprang into my mind, and I almost laughed because it was so absurd. It was crazy, but as they say, so crazy it just might work.

Here's what I came up with: when we got close to the door, I broke off from the group, so instead of them having to push me into this room, which is what they expected, I went running right in there on my own, ahead of them. Like it was the number-one place in the whole world I wanted to be. I got this big shit-eating grin on my face and I threw myself down on the bed and made myself at home. I said, "Oh wow, fellas, this is great! Is this room for me?" Like, 'you guys are real cool to make a guy feel all welcome like this.'

And these guys just froze up, as if they had no idea what to make of this weirdo in front of them. They were expecting to beat me up or rob me or whatever, and here I was acting like we're best buddies and they just did me this huge favor. So obviously I must be crazy, is what they were thinking, and it made them pause, like now they have to break their stride for a second and figure out how the hell they're gonna handle me. And so I laid it on real thick, like "Oh, look at that," you know, "you got the TV and the candles," or whatever—I don't even know what I was saying at that point, but I was making a big deal about how nice everything was and these guys were just looking at me like I was totally nuts. I had literally no idea what I was gonna do after this, what my next move was gonna be, because I had barely even thought *this* move through, let alone anything beyond that. So all of us were kind of out of ideas and it was just this weird standoff until the crowd split apart and these four dudes came into the room.

Right away I could tell these guys were some kind of authority figures. And I was right—it turned out they were the bosses (the "*capos*") of the four tanks in the corral, and I guess the accepted practice was they got first crack at the new guys, at least anyone who looked like they might have something worth some actual money. The poor junkies and the farmers and whatever, the guys who got their shit stolen right off the bat, that was okay because they didn't really have anything anyway. But everyone assumed that because I was American I must be rich, so that's why they'd brought me there.

So these guys came strolling in and you could tell they were used to getting whatever they wanted, taking it by force if it came down to that. They were some hard-looking dudes. They each had either homemade knives as long as your forearm, or else these rebar canes, like walking sticks. Pretty menacing stuff. They started jabbering away at me in Spanish, and I understood more than I let on, but I didn't want them to know that, so I just kept playing dumb, thanking them for this bitchin' room. Well, I guess they got tired of that pretty quick, because they brought this one guy in from somewhere back in the crowd, and this guy spoke English. He told me his name was Johnny, and he said he was gonna be our interpreter.

This Johnny character listened to these guys for a minute and then he turned to me and said, "Look, these guys run the show around here. You do not fuck with these guys. They like you so far, they think you got balls, but since they brought you all the way down here, they gotta take your stuff. Otherwise they're gonna lose face."

Or however he put it. He said they wanted my boots, and I said, "No way, not my boots."

"Well, you gotta give 'em something," he said.

And that's when I thought of the Levi's jacket. I had snagged it off my buddy Roger when he got sprung from the 8th Street Jail a few days before. It kept me warm enough, but it was way too small, so I was getting sick of it anyway. It was practically brand new so they were real pleased with it for two reasons: A) it was a decent jacket, and B) because it showed that they'd successfully shaken me down for something worthwhile. The natural order had been preserved, the law of the jungle. So I peeled this tiny jacket off and they went marching out of there holding it up over their heads like it was some kind of trophy, like an animal pelt, which I guess it kind of was. After catching my breath for a couple of minutes I followed them out, because I didn't want to hang around and get chased out by whoever actually lived there.

The main part of the tank, on the ground floor all around the picnic table, was filling up with people. There were some rough-looking customers eyeballing me, as well as a lot of junky-looking types just sitting around, out of it. I also caught little glimpses of a few women and kids walking through, in and out of the carracas and also along the catwalks on the upper floors. That was weird. I didn't really know what to do with myself. I figured now was as good a time as any to take a walk around the place and sort of get my bearings, so I headed for the door. I stepped outside into the corral and took a deep breath, then walked over to the gate and into the main part of the prison.

By this point it was totally dark, and people were starting to light fires around the yard. I hesitate to say it because it was still a penitentiary and I was still scared as hell, but there was almost a party atmosphere to it. I'd never seen a prison like this, never even

49

heard of one. This place was like a real little old-time Mexican village, with stores and cantinas and fruit stands and stuff like that all set up around a little square in the middle of "town." As I walked around exploring the place, I realized there were lots of families locked up in there; it seemed like everywhere you looked there was another little kid, or a woman holding a baby. It was crazy, but in a lot of ways it seemed more civilized to me than just warehousing a bunch of angry convicts in little cages. I walked through the place with my head spinning, trying to take in the whole crazy scene at once. But there was just no way—it was too weird, too foreign.

One thing that stands out in my mind to this day, in a bad way, was this young guy, maybe a few years younger than me, walking along with his mother. Maybe it was his grandmother. Anyway, she was this old lady, and she'd had a stroke or something at some point, so she was barely able to walk. And I remember her eyes just looked terrified. I don't know if she knew what was going on, but she looked like she was scared out of her mind. She couldn't talk, and her tongue was jutting out of her mouth. She made this weird *moaning* sound, just a continuous low groan, like a ghost. This kid was basically holding her up while they staggered through the yard, and with the way she looked and the noise she was making, it got under my skin and made me really uneasy. It was already dark and spooky anyway, and when they came lurching out of the shadows into the firelight, almost anything would have looked freaky, but that was bad. I still remember how awful that made me feel.

After that I was walking along, just kind of reeling, not even thinking yet about where I was going to sleep or how that would all work out, just generally freaking out about whether I'd even survive the whole experience, when I passed by this group of guys hanging around a little bonfire. One of them reached out to me as I passed and at first I flinched away from him like he was going to hit me, but then I realized he was handing me a little joint. So I kind of nodded, saying thanks, and walked on with the joint. I took a couple of good hits and it kind of took the edge off everything. Then I pinched it out and saved the roach for later. I started feeling like maybe I was going to be okay. Like there was a chance I just might make it.

Either way, it was gonna be an adventure; I knew that much for sure.

Asiento del Excusado

George Couldn't Adapt

WHEN I FIRST ARRIVED IN La Mesa, one of the first people I met was another American, this guy George Anderson. He was in there for trying to smuggle something like a million cross-tops. (Cross-tops were mini-bennies. Benzedrine. Speed. They used to be these great big tablets, but then they started making them real small with an "X" or a cross stamped into them. Cross-tops.) He'd gotten caught with the cross-tops and had immediately rolled over on his connection, who wound up being sent to the very same prison—La Mesa. So George had kind of a target on his back, and a real bad reputation as a snitch, which I didn't know about because I didn't really know about anything yet. I just knew he had a spare bunk in his carraca, which I guess should have tipped me off that he wasn't very popular. He told me I could crash there and I jumped at it. I figured out pretty quickly that he was a really unlikable guy, creepy and cocky and

53

horribly prejudiced against everybody, Mexicans especially, which, on top of everything else, didn't make him too well-liked.

At night they'd bring us all inside the tanks and lock us in, and guys would be playing guitars and playing their stereos and drinking their rice wine or their *tepache*, which was this fermented pineapple drink that was really easy to make and surprisingly not bad. And they're shooting their heroin and eating their Mandrax or whatever (Mandrax is another name for Methaqualone, which is basically like Mexican Quaaludes). Smoking their pot. Going to sleep. The real unfortunates would have nothing but a blanket, and they'd lay out a little spot on the benches, by which I mean the benches plus the table plus the floor on either side of it— just *everywhere*.

The shitter was way up front by the entrance to the tank, so if you had to go, you'd leave your carraca and have to pick your way past these guys sleeping in pretty much every inch of available space. You'd find a place to set your foot, right next to some guy's head, and then try to balance there while you found your next spot, maybe just missing another guy's fingers. Sometimes to get there you'd have to climb up onto the table and then down the other side, back and forth, finding these little stepping stones of empty space where you weren't going to walk on somebody and piss them off. It was not easy.

And when you finally got there, of course, it was a total fiasco. It wasn't quite a third-world-hole-in-the-ground toilet, but pretty close. Imagine basically a toilet bowl with no seat on it and no tank to flush it with. So what you'd do is you'd sort of balance on the rim of this thing while you squatted down, and then when you were done, there was this 55-gallon barrel of water there with a dip can, like a gallon can on a chain, and you'd scoop out enough water to flush the toilet.

Anyway, what this guy George had, that he was just so proud of, was this disgusting old shit-splattered toilet seat that he'd gotten from somewhere or other, which he kept hanging up on a nail in his carraca. Whenever he had to go—he'd be wearing his robe, this red plaid robe, and he'd go marching through the tank with this toilet seat tucked under his arm like he was some kind of general or lord or something. He had stringy blond hair and a pot belly and skinny white legs. Every time I saw him marching through there with his toilet seat, I couldn't help laughing; he looked ridiculous. He thought he was so much better than everybody else and yet he just looked like an idiot. If you find yourself in a new situation, you have to adapt, right? He couldn't do it.

This is awful, but one time I remember George got dysentery. If you've ever had dysentery, you know that it makes you shit pretty much constantly; it's horrible. Somebody was always getting dysentery because the water and the food and everything was so filthy and contaminated. Anyway, so George got it, and one night he was doing his thing, marching from his carraca up to the front with his little robe and his toilet seat under his arm, and as he got more and more desperate, he started going faster and faster and faster, picking his way through these people sleeping all over the benches until he was practically running...

...and about halfway there, it *broke loose*. It just got away from him; he was shitting like a goose. He was fully sprinting now, just running and shitting, running and shitting, all over these guys, just letting it go. Everyone was waking up and realizing what had happened to them, but by then he was long gone, shitting on other people. Finally, he made it to the end and cleaned himself up a little bit in the bathroom and then snuck back the other way while all these people were groaning, like, "Oh, God!"

I'm sorry. It's disgusting, but it's real.

Mansión

A Place of My Own

ONE OF THE FIRST FRIENDS I made, and easily the best friend I had my whole time inside, was this guy called Johnny Bigotes. (Johnny was the interpreter my first night in there, when the capos were shaking me down for my jacket.) *"Bigotes"* means mustache—Johnny Mustache. He was also known as Juan Salcido, and also Johnny Ellis. I believe there were others. Why did he have so many aliases? I never asked him; I guess he felt it was necessary. Johnny was a real nice guy, instantly friendly to everybody and everybody liked him. He'd done time in an American prison or two before La Mesa, and by the time I met him he was pretty well institutionalized. I remember one time we were hanging around by the outside gate, and we saw this early-sixties car drive by. I think it was a Chevy Malibu, maybe, like about a '62; it was okay, nothing special. And Johnny goes, "Wow, Steve, look at the new Chevy!" This was 1974. He thought a twelve-year-old

57

car was brand new. That's the kind of weird time-perception thing that happens to people who are in prison too long. The world sort of moves on without you. He also wore clothes—dress pants, loafers, collared shirts—that were eight or ten years out of style.

Anyway, the reason I bring up Johnny is, after my first few nights on George Anderson's spare bed, I was pretty antsy to line up my own carraca, and I figured Johnny might be able to help me with it. I was starting to hear the rumors about George: how he was a snitch, he was a creep, whatever, and I definitely got that vibe off of him; it was time to go. Plus he hung that toilet seat of his on a nail right over my bunk. It was definitely time to go.

Johnny himself had actually come up to me in the corral one day and just kind of whispered as he was walking by that I shouldn't get too friendly with George. Like he was bad news, and he was gonna make me look bad, too. At first you don't trust anybody in prison, you don't believe anything, because you don't know who's trying to scam you or trick you or whatever. But the more I got to know George and to see him in action, the more I started figuring out that Johnny was right. George was a creep, and nobody liked him; he didn't have any friends. So I appreciated Johnny looking out for me like that.

Something they did every morning, early, when the sun was just peeking over the wall, was the guards would come storming through the tanks, banging their billy clubs against the carracas and yelling "*Lista! Lista! La cuenta!*" The count. We'd drag our asses out to the corral, and everybody would stand around with the other people from their tank while the guards took a head count. It took forever, and it was almost always freezing. Guys would build fires with whatever they could find around: plastic or old tires, sometimes wood, and we'd huddle around in that toxic smoke and try to get warm.

So on maybe my third or fourth day, they woke us up for lista, and we were all out in the corral, and I went looking for Johnny. Finally I saw him and I walked over and said, "Fuckin' A, you were right about that George guy. I gotta get out of there." So he said he could help me get a place, said he'd introduce me to Heladio Diaz.

Well I won't lie, my sphincter kind of squinched when he said that, because that was a pretty serious name. Everybody knew Heladio Diaz; even on the outside you heard about him. There were *songs* about Heladio Diaz. He was a big-time drug boss, and I heard that on the day they busted him, he had an eleven-hour gun battle with the federales before they were finally able to bring him down. He was known for being absolutely fearless. In here, he was the head capo of the whole place; he was like The Godfather. He got ten percent of everything that went on in the prison—everything. If you sold ten papers of *chiva*, which is what they called heroin, you kicked one down to him. Shit, if you sold ten tacos, you kicked one down to him, or the cash equivalent anyway. He was a scary, powerful dude. If you wanted to do anything in La Mesa, you had to go through Heladio, and that included real estate, because even though the tanks were these total shantytowns, they still had actual paper deeds to every carraca. You had to buy it, you couldn't just strongarm a guy out of his place. I guess that's how they kept the peace, and how they made sure Heladio got his cut. No way around it—everything went through him.

Johnny offered to introduce me to him, so of course I said sure, and later that day he took me over to Heladio's place. Now, you picture a normal carraca, right? This wasn't that. This was a two-story *casa* looking out over the square. It had a little balcony up top with a Jacuzzi on it, and sometimes at the fiestas you'd see Heladio up there with his bodyguards and his entourage, which was usually these two beautiful girls and this one sort of flamboyant pretty boy, and they'd all be drinking and dancing and whatever. There was always a lot of gossip and rumors around about Heladio and his people, about their alcohol and their drugs and their sex practices, especially.

So we climbed up the stairs and there was this steel security gate like you see in shitty neighborhoods, and then behind that there was a normal door with one of those slidey kind of peepholes. Johnny banged on the security gate and a second later the peephole slid open and someone looked out. Johnny said he wanted to see about a carraca and the peephole slid shut. Then the door opened up and Heladio himself was standing there with a big smile on his face. He was wearing a pale green *guayabera* and white slacks. Bare feet. He looked more European than Mexican, more like a dapper old-school Spaniard or an

Italian gentleman. He had great hair, black with a cool streak of white in the front. Just a real distinguished-looking dude. Anyway, he didn't even look at me at first, but he was warm and friendly to Johnny: shook his hand, asked him how he was doing, all that. Then Johnny introduced me. He said, "This is Steve," and Heladio turned to me, and I swear my blood ran cold. I can't explain it; he didn't do anything, it was just the force of him. I could feel my life in his hands. But I did what I always did: I played it cool.

"How you doin'?" I said. He just smiled at me. And then, what really freaked me out is, he said to Johnny,

"Okay, you can go."

So Johnny turned to me and he said, like, "Good luck" or whatever, and he just left me there! Now I was freaked out, because even though Heladio was all friendly and smiling at the moment, I'd heard all these stories about how he was so ruthless and he was a killer and he was this and he was that. But he waved me inside and what was I supposed to do? I had to go in.

I followed him inside and he had this full living room set up in there. It was really nice and you could see he had an office area and his bedroom was in the back with the balcony off of that. There was a girl in the bed, partially covered by a white satin sheet. I could see her blonde hair and olive skin, and she looked good. I didn't want to be gawking at her, but she looked really good. And right in front of me, in the living room, he had two more of his playthings or whatever you want to call them. At one end of the black leather couch was the young homosexual kid wearing this big white robe with light blue slippers. There was a cigarette dangling from his hand, and I remember the ash was real long and I kept looking at it, waiting for it to fall, but I want to say it never did. At the other end of the couch was a girl, and she was *beautiful*. Black hair, dark skin, I'd say she was about seventeen years old. She was wearing a short tight black skirt and a black lace bra, and she had a gold bracelet that she was playing with, sort of dangling it between her lips. Very seductive. Heladio introduced me to the girl first. She slid the bracelet back onto her wrist, almost like she was embarrassed, and stood up to shake my hand. She smiled at me, looked me right in my eyes. Her name was Elsa. The boy was called Bobby. He didn't get up, he just nodded from the couch, so I nodded back. Then Heladio told me to take a seat. There was a glass coffee table in front of the couch with a chair at one end of it. I sat in the chair while Heladio sat down between Elsa and Bobby.

"You would like a carraca," he said.

"Yeah, I would. Tank C if possible."

Tank C was where most of the Americans stayed. There were better apartments in the buildings outside of the corral, but Americans weren't allowed to stay in them since a bunch of them had escaped not long before. He nodded, as if to say it was no big deal, then he turned to Elsa and said something in Spanish that I didn't catch. She got up and poured us a couple of drinks from a bar in the corner. Tequila, really nice, in fancy crystal glasses. Meanwhile, Heladio opened this silver and mother-of-pearl snuff box that was sitting in front of him and poured out a good-sized little pile of cocaine right onto the glass table. And then he pulled out a pack of cigarettes (Fiesta brand, I believe) and offered me one. I've never been a smoker so I said no, but he took one for himself and gently mashed the tip of it into the cocaine, then lit it up. That was a trick I'd seen a lot of the Mexican bigshots do with coke or heroin, sometimes both. He took a long drag of that and then he started cutting up lines with a razor blade. Five lines he cut.

There was an end table with a drawer in it, and Heladio reached past Bobby and pulled it open. Inside I could see a stack of hundred-dollar bills and a Browning nine-millimeter. He peeled a hundred off the stack and closed the drawer. Then he rolled up the bill and offered it to me. I said, "Ladies first," and so he handed it to Elsa. She made quick work of her line and then it was my turn. I snorted mine and then Heladio did his and then it was Bobby's turn. I don't know if his nasal passages were clogged or what the problem was but he just couldn't make it work so he ended up eating his coke. That left one line for the other girl, the one in the bedroom. She came in with the sheet wrapped around her, and if anything she was even hotter than Elsa. She was older, maybe early twenties, and just ridiculously gorgeous. The way she had it draped, the sheet barely covered her, and she just kept looking at me and smiling. She did her line no problem and the whole time, she kept smiling at me. I think she knew how nervous she was making me; I think that was the point. They said her name was Irma.

We finished our drinks and took a walk, just me and Heladio. I didn't see any bodyguards, but I couldn't really tell. He might have had guys looking out for him all along the way, hanging back in the crowd. We went through the yard to the corral and then over to C Tank. I noticed how quickly everyone got out of his way. Anyhow, we went through the tank to the back where the stairs were and then up to the second floor and took a left on the rickety catwalk. Heladio stopped next to one carraca and said,

"This is the place."

I looked inside: it was about seven feet deep by maybe six feet wide. There was no door. The floor was uneven and covered in rat turds, and it felt like you could step right through the rotten boards into the carraca below. Nothing was cut to fit, it was just scrap plywood and boards sort of patchworked together, everything overlapping. The walls were made of cardboard, newspaper and termite-chewed wood with gaps here and there where you could see through to the neighbors' rooms. And there were about half a dozen dead bodies piled on the floor. Actually it turned out they weren't dead, just passed out from sniffing glue or acetone or something. There was a jar open on the floor, and it gave off a strong chemical smell.

But the place had a window! In the back, up near the ceiling, there was an open window with bars on it. It was about five feet long and a foot and a half high. Even with everything else wrong with the place, the fresh air from that window would make it feel like a palace. I asked him how much. Two hundred and fifty bucks, he said, and it was the only carraca for sale anywhere. I had no choice. I turned away from him and dug my money out of my stash.

(When you're in prison, or you hang around people who've been in prison, you learn pretty quickly the best places to hide things. The first place anybody's gonna look for your valuables is in your pockets, and then in your socks, but if you know what you're doing, the better hiding place is inside the waistband of your jeans. What you do is you make a vertical slit through the inside layer of the waistband, and that gives you access to the little pocket between that and the outer layer, and that runs all the way around your waist. Sometimes it's divided where the belt loops are sewn on, but then you just need to cut more slits to get at the other compartments. That can be handy anyway to keep your stash separated, your drugs from your money, or your small bills from your large bills or what have you. There you go: free advice!)

Anyway, Roger had brought me a few hundred in cash before they transferred me out of La Ocho, so I counted out Heladio's money and gave it to him. He handed me the deed to the room and explained the rules: the place belonged to me until I either got out or died. If I wanted to sell it before then, I had to go through him. Somehow I expected that. I pointed at the pile of guys passed out on the floor.

"Do they come with the place?"

He laughed and poked them with his foot to wake them up. Then he gave them each a little dollar paper of chiva and they all ran off to go fix. We shook hands and he was on his way.

So there I was in my new home, and man, was it ever a shithole. It needed a lot of work. First on the list was a door. There was a small garbage dump out behind the corral where you could scrounge all sorts of random junk from out of the burning piles. When I got there and started looking around, I saw the tank capo who'd taken my Levi's jacket the first night. He was wearing it. He spotted me and tried to sell it back to me for two dollars, but I told him he should keep it; I said it looked good on him. It didn't, he looked stupid, but it was funny to see how shocked he was that I didn't want it back. At the dump I found a couple of old soda-pop crates and some boards that I figured I could use to build a door. I dragged my treasures back to the tank and wrestled them up the stairs to my carraca. I was starting to feel a little bit sick, so I wanted to get a door on the place before it got too bad. I wanted the privacy.

Just about then, Johnny Bigotes came in and looked around at the place. He nodded like he approved, like it wasn't too bad. He asked if I needed any help building the door. I told him I could definitely use some help, so he disappeared for a few minutes and came back with a hammer and a saw and a little bag of nails. He had a couple of mismatched hinges, too, so together we built the door and hung it. It looked pretty good. (At first I used a bent nail to hold it shut; later on I bought a small lock off a guy.)

By this time I was feeling pretty shitty. I knew I was running a fever and my guts were going crazy. I had a thin mattress in there (whether it came with the place or Johnny brought it I don't remember), so I closed the door and laid down on that. Even though I figured I was probably coming down with dysentery, in a way I felt better. If I was gonna get sick and die, at least now I had my own place to do it in.

Not long after I flopped down there on the floor, basically resigning myself to whatever was gonna become of me, I heard a huge commotion downstairs in the tank, so I had to get up again and check it out. I dragged myself out the door and onto the little catwalk, thinking the whole time that I was gonna pitch over the side and die, as dizzy as I was. Looking down, I saw a big brawl going off on the ground floor next to the picnic table right below me.

It was Mexicans versus Americans, a bunch of them on each side. The Americans were fighting them off with clubs and fists and whatever else they had, but they were badly outnumbered, and all I could think was, "Shit, they're gonna kill us all and I can't even fight." I couldn't do anything, so I just went back inside and flopped down on my mattress again, waiting for them to come and get me if that's what they were gonna do. But I guess it came to a head and then everybody dispersed and that was the end of it. I never did find out what the problem was.

So I'm laying there and I'm sicker than hell and I can't eat anything, can't drink anything. (Not that I wanted to; the only water they had was this funky-ass cloudy water where you could actually see stuff floating on top, and eventually you reach a point where you're so thirsty you don't even care about that, but I wasn't quite at that point yet.) So I just laid there when I wasn't puking in a can, which I spent a good portion of my time doing, and tried to sleep, but all around me I kept hearing this scratching, skittering noise: *rats*.

There was a little bit of light coming in from the window at the back and also through the gaps in the boards at the top of the front wall, above the door. Every time I heard them I'd open my eyes and find them trying to climb on me, to bite me or to get at the puke in the can by my head. And each time I'd yell or stomp my foot to scare them away. Eventually I took my boots off so I could throw them at them or use one as a hammer to smack 'em or just bang the floorboards to chase them off. I remember there was one entire night where I didn't get even a wink of sleep because I had to spend the entire time dealing with these little fuckers. That was about the low point of my life at the time.

After a few days my health turned the corner. I fought through it and fought through it, and slowly I started getting better. One of the families that lived in the tank brought me some food which also helped a lot. (In that way, La Mesa was like a real little community. I think about someone in an American prison looking out for a stranger

68

like that and it seems pretty far-fetched, to say the least.)

Once I was up and around again, I set to work really tricking out my carraca. If I was going to spend the rest of my life in this place, which seemed as likely as not, I figured I might as well make it as comfortable as I could. I gave it a lot of thought and then I had Roger bring me down some wood and some paint and a couple of big paisley tapestries, which were easy to come by back in the hippie days. So Roger showed up and he had three cans of paint, but all three of them were these little dinky cans that weren't nearly enough to do anything with on their own, and they were all different colors. So I ended up mixing them all together which gave me kind of a muddy blue color, and I used that to paint the ceiling and the back wall. I left the front wall pretty much how it was because it was in the best shape, and I tacked the tapestries up along the side walls. I took special care to nail those down tight in the corners and along the floor, thinking it might help to keep the rats and the bugs from getting in.

At some point in there I got my hands on a metal army cot to go with my thin little mattress. I don't recall exactly how that came about, but that was a major score. And that gave me the idea to try to maximize my living space by elevating my bed right up under the window like a sleeping loft. I was so excited I didn't even really measure it that carefully; I just nailed up the posts I planned to rest the bed on and then hoisted the cot up on to them. I put it in on an angle so I could get the two legs at the head of the bed onto the braces and then I was gonna lower it gently down onto the other two. But when I started to lower it down I got a sick feeling in the pit of my stomach—it didn't fit.

It turned out the bed was about an inch longer than the room was wide. And because it was made with these heavy metal bars, there was no way I could cut it to fit or even bend it to get it in there. At that point I'd be goddamned if I was gonna reorient the thing to run along the side wall or any shit like that; I was dead set on putting my bed up under that window. So what I did was I climbed up on something with my hammer in my hand and I just pounded the shit out of that bed until I managed to push the neighbors' wall over far enough to get the bed level. I don't know how I pulled that off without attracting the whole tank with the clatter I was making, but I did. I had my loft, and underneath it I placed another little mattress covered with another tapestry, sort of like a Bedouin couch, which were real popular at the time.

Then along the side wall to the right of the door when you walked in, I propped up a board, which was already painted yellow, on some bricks or something to make a little bench. That's where I would eat sometimes. If I was lucky enough to get my hands on some peanut butter and jelly, say, I'd sit there on that little bench and make my sandwich, resting the bread directly on the leg of my jeans because I don't think I ever did have any plates.

Yeah, ████████ it was pretty rough. But it was home.

Toro

Bull's-Head Tacos
and the Salad Dog

ONE OF THE REALLY MESSED-UP facts of life in La Mesa for me was that even though I was locked up in a state penitentiary, I was technically a federal prisoner, since I was there on federal charges. What this meant is that the state authorities who ran the place were under no direct obligation to feed me, so they didn't. What I got was the equivalent of seven dollars every two weeks from the federales, and out of that seven dollars I was supposed to buy food and whatever else I needed. As you can imagine, it didn't go far, so if I wanted to eat, I had to get creative.

Working in the prison shops—wood shop, welding, that kind of stuff—was an option, but for the kind of kid I was, and the situation I was in, it was certainly no option for me. There was no way I could get my head around

73

the idea of lifting a finger to help the people who had me locked up, even if it meant I would starve. I just couldn't do it. In fact, I even bought my way out of work detail when I first arrived in La Mesa. There was a policy in place at the time that said that all new inmates had to do a mandatory period of work in the prison industries. I forget how long it was, but because that system was just as corrupt as every other in there, you had the unspoken option of buying your way out of it, so that's what I did. I think it was fifteen dollars or something like that. It was well worth it to me not to have to work. Stealing, likewise, wasn't even an option. There's actually very little theft in prison, in my experience anyway. The risk is just way too great. Someone is bound to find out, and it's not like you can make a clean getaway.

Sometimes I'd get a bit of cash from friends who'd come in to see me, and I had my seven dollars from the feds, but I always tried to stretch my money and make it last a little longer. It didn't always work out.

One time I remember I was just starving, my ribs were sticking out; I was dizzy. I don't think I'd eaten anything for at least a couple of days. (All told, I think I lost somewhere in the neighborhood of fifty pounds while I was in there, and I wasn't real chubby to begin with. Between the dysentery and the damn starvation, that was a pretty effective diet plan to say the least.) I had no money to speak of, but I could still get credit. That was never a problem in La Mesa; as long as you were willing to put your life down for collateral, you could buy most anything on credit. Those terms made the deal a lot less attractive, though. I never liked to be in debt to anybody, especially not like that, but these were desperate times.

Well, right down the street not far from the prison was the arena where they held bullfights every Sunday. The bulls always lost, which was unfortunate for them but lucky for a lot of us in the prison because their heads usually wound up in the giant cooking pot of this one inmate chef; I forget his name. The first time I had *cabeza* tacos, I was walking through the yard one day, just starving, and I saw these guys with a huge black cooking pot sitting in the fire. There's steam coming out of it, and the smell was just incredible. I swear it was like a cartoon, where you see the guy kind of floating along on the vapors of whatever good thing he's smelling—that was me. So I followed my nose, I went floating over there, and I saw them lift the lid and inside of it there was this gigantic bull's head. They'd sawed the horns off to make it fit in the pot, but damn if it wasn't a full-on bull's head sitting there, just bubbling away. The guy was throwing all sorts of stuff in there with it: onions, salt, pepper, cilantro, and my stomach was just in knots because even though it was totally gross to think about it, and definitely not something I would have eaten on the outside if I had any choice about it, at the time it just smelled so good to me I thought I was either gonna cry or pass out.

The guy saw me looking at him, and looking at this pot boiling there, and he asked me if I wanted a taco. So there I was nodding away until he asked me if I had any money. Well, I didn't, so I had to just shake my head. I could see him thinking for a second, like he was considering his options, and then in the end he carved some of this meat off this thing— the cheek, I think it was—and he put it in a warm flour tortilla and topped it off with some really good salsa and then he handed it to me. It was twenty-five cents, but he said I could pay him later. I think he knew how hungry I was and took pity on me. So I ate the bull's head taco, and it was every bit as good as it smelled. I'm not sure I'd eat another one if you put it in front of me right now, but at the time, in the state I was in, it was absolutely perfect.

There were other delicacies I tried, too. Nothing as out-there as the tacos, but good stuff. One was watermelon with chili powder on it, which is how they eat a lot of fruit down there in Mexico, but I'd never tried it before. There was one dude who had the fruit concession there and he always had this great big machete with him. He was in there for murder. I didn't know the circumstances of his case but I assumed it had something to do with that machete because he seemed awfully attached to it. Anyway, you could go up to this guy's stand and buy yourself some watermelon and he would whip out that machete and chop you off a hunk before you could even blink your eyes. Real neat slices, and always super-fast; he was an expert with that blade. Then he'd sprinkle the chili powder on it, and that was the thing right there. That was a treat. Something else this guy had that was kind of cool was, if you wanted orange juice, he had this hand-cranked orange juice machine. I've never seen another one like it, so I wonder if maybe this guy invented it, but it was this heavy-duty handle thing that he'd crank around and it would press the oranges and also turn them at the same time so he could get every bit of juice out of them. No electric power or anything, all mechanical. So you got fresh orange juice; that was pretty neat.

But as I said, finding my next meal was pretty much a constant concern. The thing that totally saved me, that I came to depend on, was the hot dog stand. The guy who ran it sold these little hot dogs, just your basic little wieners, for around twenty cents, I think. And he'd let me buy on credit. So I'd get my little twenty-cent hot dog—basic dog, basic bun— and then he had all the condiments there, and that's where I'd get creative. I used to literally pile on the onions and peppers—I'd line the peppers up end-to-end and stack them so it was like I was building a brick wall of peppers—and then I'd add relish and tomatoes and whatever else he had that day. By the time I got finished raiding this guy's condiments I'd have the garnish literally stacked two or three inches high over the top of the bun; it was like a big salad with a little dinky hot dog buried underneath it. That was my salvation; I ate a *lot* of salad dogs that year.

Sombrero

Yosemite Sam
and the Laundry Girls

ONE REALLY BIZARRE SIGHT AT la cuenta, but also fascinating in a weird way, were the transvestites. There were maybe ten or twelve of them who were really going for it, the cross-dressing. Some of them actually cleaned up pretty good, but in the mornings they all just looked like hell. I mean *obvious dudes*, with stubble and crooked wigs and their makeup all smeared, but wearing ladies' nightgowns and even lingerie, some of them. Just horrible-looking.

They always had this one old guy with them, and he sort of ran herd on all these girls; he was their pimp. He let them stay in his carraca with him, and he was obviously having sex with them, but he looked like the straightest guy you could ever meet. I remember he had a wide black mustache, like a Hitler-style mustache, but bigger. It looked like a comb stuck to his lip. And he wore this great big—I mean *gigantic*—cowboy hat. It was almost like a novelty hat, like it wasn't even supposed to be a serious hat. Like a cartoon cowboy hat. He looked like Yosemite Sam from Bugs Bunny. A Mexican Yosemite Sam.

One thing that was interesting is this old cowboy guy not only lived with these transvestites and pimped them out or whatever, he also ran the laundry business. You'd drop your clothes off, or they'd have a kid come by and pick them up, and the transvestites would do your laundry. There were these big concrete troughs in the corral and they had these old-timey washboards, and they'd just be scrubbing clothes all day when they weren't turning tricks or whatever. They did everybody's laundry, everyone with money anyway, and they did a good job. A lot of the guards used them, even.

That old cowboy had a good thing going, I think; he did all right for himself.

Diamante

Treasures In the Minefield

EVERYTHING WAS SO DIRTY AND filthy, and everyone was packed in so tight with their neighbors, that just trying not to get seriously ill was pretty much a full-time job. There were all kinds of nasty illnesses going around, like dysentery and tuberculosis. Some weeks it seemed like half the people in there had TB. It was horrible. You could lie in your bed at night and hear people coughing all over the prison, in every tank, that gross wet chunky kind of cough.

When you walked through the corral or the yard or anywhere, you had to be careful where you stepped because guys were always spitting up these horrible clumps of bloody mucus. They'd spit it out wherever they were; they didn't care. This stuff was just deadly, though. You'd be almost guaranteed to get infected if it got into you. I used to think of walking around there almost like I was

walking through a minefield, which I
basically was, I guess, when you consider that
a wrong step could literally cost you your life.
The only difference was the death would be
slower and probably more painful. So you
had to watch out for the mucus and make sure
that you didn't step in it.

One unexpected benefit to all this walking
around looking at the ground was discovering
little jewels, like little rhinestones and shirt
buttons and stuff like that kind of glittering in
the dirt. I never really gave much thought to
where they came from. I guess they maybe
fell off the transvestites, or if there was a
fight or something they might have been torn
off somebody's cowboy shirt. But from time to
time I'd be walking through the yard trying
not to step on the death blobs of poison
phlegm and I would find these little sparkly
things.

For some reason they made me happy. Maybe
it was just the idea of finding some beauty in
such an ugly place; maybe it was the thrill of
coming across something kind of rare, like a
four-leaf clover. Whatever the reason, I liked
them, and I started to collect them. I
remember the first one I found was a
rhinestone that still had the little metal
prongs on the back of it. I stuck it on my
jeans, on the front pocket. That way, I could
look at it whenever I wanted. Over the course
of my time in La Mesa I probably collected
about a dozen more of these things in
different sizes and colors and styles, all stuck
onto my Levi's, sort of half to mark the time,
and half just to give me something nice to
look at when things got especially depressing.

I don't have those jeans any more, but I wish I did. They would make a good souvenir to remind me of how I dealt with that place, how I survived it.

Cuchara

Doctór and the Hot Sauce Cure

THEY CALLED HIM "*DOCTÓR*," ALL right, but let me tell you, this guy was no doctor. He was just this kind of hunched-over-looking guy with long, greasy hair under a little fedora, and he always had a bandana hanging around his neck. Something to know about bandanas: you'd see them all over the place, I mean almost everybody had one, but they used them for different things. First off there were so many stabbings going on all the time that guys would use them to bandage themselves up; you saw that a lot. Some guys would tie them around their necks like cowboys for whatever reason—I guess they thought it looked cool. A few people wore them like headbands, because almost everybody at the time had long hair. But mostly what you'd see were guys with bandanas draped around their necks, or hanging over their shoulders. What that meant was those guys were waiting to score some chiva. When they got ahold of some, they'd use the bandana to tie off, you know, to make their vein swell up so they could shoot it. Anyway, Doctór was one of them who wore it draped like that, and he also ran the Shooting Gallery. That's what they called the room where everybody went to shoot up. The shooting gallery was this guy's carraca, and it was on the ground floor in Tank C, where I had my place.

Whenever anybody would get their hands on some chiva they'd go to the shooting gallery to fix. You'd see them lined up outside, and the line would snake around the tank, and they were also lined up inside. I mean there might be twenty or thirty guys lined up at a time. And they'd take turns shooting up. The Doctór, who ran the place, had needles and syringes and stuff, everything you needed, and he was real good at finding the vein, which a lot of these guys had trouble with because their veins were simply blown out from doing it so much. Forgive the gross details here, but they'd have this sore on their arm that looked almost like a little volcano, just scab on top of scab on top of scab, and what they'd do is they'd peel back the top of it and then jam the needle into the hole and kind of poke it around until they hit the vein. And that's what Doctór was so good at; he had the touch.

Anyway, so they'd wait their turn and then when they got to the front of the line, Doctór would shoot them up. He would take their little bindle, their little paper of chiva, and he'd cook it in a spoon over a candle with some drops of water. Sometimes instead of a spoon he'd use the metal cap off a big soda bottle, with a piece of wire twisted around it to make a kind of handle, so it looked like a miniature frying pan. He'd tie them off and then he'd get it all ready and he'd inject them. And for doing this, his price was two drops from every syringe. Before he gave them their fix he'd take the syringe and poke it into this vial and squeeze out two drops, and then the rest he'd shoot into the guy. Believe me when I say they watched him like a hawk; it was always exactly two drops. But it added up: Doctór was fucked up pretty much all the time. It was a profitable business for him.

So one day this visitor came in, this American—white guy—and he was a stone cold junky. He was a mess, so he scored some chiva and then his buddies or whoever he was in there to see took him to Doctór to get him fixed up. He did his thing, and he came walking out into the corral, all smiles, and then he just kind of... fell over. Just collapsed there on the ground. Overdose. He looked dead; this guy was a goner. And so everybody was going apeshit because just think about how this looks: Here you are trying to run a prison, and now you've got, not even an inmate, a visitor—even worse, an *American* visitor—overdosing on heroin that he bought right there inside of the prison. I mean, this is a major scandal shaping up here. Of course everyone was freaking out because if this guy didn't sign out at the end of the day, they'd know he was dead and then the warden would be embarrassed and it would be this big fiasco and the first thing they'd do after that is shut down the shooting gallery and throw Doctór in the *tumbas* (which means "tombs," which is what they called solitary confinement). That's if they didn't just kill him, because they had that option, too.

So these guys were trying to revive their buddy, they were slapping his face, and everybody was in total panic mode, but the guy was just *gone*. Somebody ran back inside to get Doctór, and he came running out and looked at the guy, and he just about had a heart attack because he thought the guy was done for, too. The guy really did look dead; he looked like he had already expired. Everyone was freaking out, but Doctór looked at him hard for a second and then he said, "No! I can save heem!"

He sprinted back inside, and everybody jumped out of his way because they wanted to see what he was gonna do, like "How's he gonna save this guy?" And he came running back out with a syringe and what looked like a bottle of Tabasco sauce. I mean it looked exactly like one of those miniature bottles of hot sauce; he said it was his own special concoction, his own special antidote. He stuck the needle into the bottle and pulled some of this stuff out and jammed it into the guy's arm. Then he hit the plunger, and immediately, I mean IMMEDIATELY, this guy sat straight up like he'd just sat up in his coffin. And sweat just came pouring—like *shooting*—out of this guy, out of his face, out of his arms, everywhere, like he was on fire. And he jumped up and spun around and was like,

"What the fuck!? Where the fuck am I?!"

Then he went running off back toward the gate and we never saw him again. Everyone laughed, even though if you think about what had just happened, it really wasn't that funny. It was just kind of comical to see the guy jump up and run away like that. I think it was nervous laughter more than anything.

Anyway, as the crowd broke up I took a peek at the little bottle of antidote. Turned out it actually *was* hot sauce. That's it—he just shot him full of hot sauce and the damn guy lived.

Pistola

Shootout At the Corral

WHEN YOU WALKED INTO MY tank, Tank C, you passed directly under this sort of balcony in the front of the tank. This is on the inside, at the end of the catwalk on the second floor, and it overlooked the main area of the tank where the long picnic table was. There was an old black-and-white TV up on a ledge on the balcony and every afternoon a lot of the tank guys and, I want to say, most of the kids would gather around and watch "Popeye the Sailor Man." They would sit at that end of the picnic table looking up at the TV and they would all sing along, I swear to God. It was the funniest scene: dozens of these total cutthroat junkies, murderers, transvestites, weirdos and little kids all singing along with Popeye at the top of their lungs, just loving it.

One day it was almost time for "Popeye" and I was sort of wandering through the corral; I think I was going out for a hot dog or something. I had just left the tank and was maybe halfway through the corral when a gunfight broke out. I was trapped right in the middle of it. There were a lot of people milling around when all of a sudden two guys started shooting at each other, one on either side of the crowd.

So the bullets were whizzing by and we were all running back and forth like crazy, because these guys were just squeezing off shots, barely even looking where they were aiming. I don't know what their beef was, but they were determined to settle it right then and there. They ran around in a big circle trying to get away from each other, and the whole time they were sort of reaching back and firing their guns as they ran. It was like they thought they were going to outrun the bullets or something. Of course I and everybody else were trying to get out of there as fast as we could, but there were a lot of panicking people there and so we made a big traffic jam, like a bottleneck, at the gate that led out of the corral. We were trying to get all skinny and sideways, just praying we didn't catch a loose bullet. And these two guys literally ran in circles shooting at each other until they had both emptied their guns. When they had no more bullets left to shoot, they ran away in opposite directions, and that was it. Nobody got shot; even though there were bullets flying everywhere, not a single person was hit. It was a miracle.

When the dust settled, everyone looked around at each like we couldn't believe we'd survived, and then we all went back in the tank and watched "Popeye" as if nothing strange had happened. Crazy.

Palmera

Fiesta of the Greased Pole

THE MEXICAN CULTURE IS ABSOLUTELY crazy for parties; they'll throw a party for any reason at all, any chance they get. That's one of the main things that made my time in La Mesa bearable. Almost every weekend there was some kind of celebration going on, and it made it feel less like a prison.

One of the biggest ones I remember happened not too long after I arrived. I forget the occasion. As usual, they woke us up early for lista, and then everybody went back to bed for a while. When I got up a little while later it was still pretty early, but there were already visitors arriving and the place seemed busier than usual for that time of the morning.

I went for a walk, going about my business, looking for a taco or whatever, and I saw these guys out in the middle of the soccer field, digging a hole. 'That's odd,' I thought. So I watched them for a while. And then I looked and I saw they had a telephone pole lying on the ground there next to them. Now it was getting really weird. So I wandered over there, you know, to find out what the hell was going on, and I saw these other guys with this big hammer—not quite a sledgehammer, but a big hammer—and they were pounding lengths of rebar, maybe three-eighths-inch rebar, into the end of the telephone pole. The rebar was about two and a half, three feet long, and they were pounding them in and then bending them over, so it kind of looked like a palm tree now.

I was thinking these guys were just nuts, like they were gonna try to jazz up the place with their fake palm tree right in the middle of the soccer field, and I was just about to walk away, to write them off and walk away, when they came out with this pail of *manteca*, which is lard, and started rubbing it all over the telephone pole. Just greasing the hell out of this telephone pole with the lard. So now, of course, this was amazing. This was getting really weird. What the hell were these guys up to?!

By now I was hooked, and I wasn't going anywhere until I found out what these nuts were doing. But meanwhile, in the background, I saw these other guys—this is over by the basketball court—I saw these other guys, and they were setting up a wrestling ring! How did I know it was a wrestling ring and not a boxing ring? Because they had masks on. I swear to God, they were these big musclebuilder dudes, and they had on these Mexican wrestling masks. (*Lucha* masks, they called them. And when the masks were on, these guys stayed in character. There were a number of wrestlers locked up in the prison and you never knew it; they just seemed like everybody else. But some days, like this one, they'd put their masks on and set up their ring, and they were like celebrities in there. They were like superheroes.)

This was my first time seeing the wrestler guys, so of course I was like, "Holy shit, I gotta check *that* out." I started to head over there, when I heard this big cheer go up behind me. I turned around and I saw one of the really big-time capos coming over from his apartment with his entourage. He had like six guys with him, and they were marching over to where these guys were greasing the telephone pole. Everybody was crowding around and cheering and clapping as they passed by. At this point I looked around and realized the place was really filling up. There were a lot of visitors there by now, and they were all dressed up fancy, and a lot of them had picnic baskets and bags of food and stuff, and it was just a real festive atmosphere.

So anyway, this capo walked over to the pole and he started digging in his pockets, and he had a roll of string and he started tying stuff onto the rebar palm fronds. He had cash and little papers of chiva, papers of cocaine, rolls of pot. He tied these things on there while his bodyguards stood around guarding it, and the people just went nuts. They cheered and clapped, then another capo came out and it got even louder. This guy was a little more big-time than the first guy, and he came over with his entourage, all smiling and waving to the crowd, and he tied his stuff on there. When he was done another one came out. They went through maybe five or six of these guys, and then the last one was Heladio. When he came out, forget it, people just *lost* it. They knew he was gonna put something really good on the tree, so they were jumping up and down and hooting and hollering, and he smiled and shook their hands. He tied his stuff on and then it was time to stand the pole up. They got some ropes on the end of it and hoisted until it was standing in the hole, then they packed the dirt down around it. By now there were a few hundred people gathered around, and the anticipation was just insane. Everybody'd been partying, half the prison was drunk off their ass or high on one thing or another, the visitors were having a great time, there were pretty girls everywhere, the wrestlers were doing their flips and shit, putting on a show, there were bands now— actual mariachi bands walking around playing their instruments—everybody was dancing, and it was just a full-on party scene. It was incredible! And now it was time for the high point of the whole fiesta.

The way it worked was, there were several different groups of junkies, different *cliquas*, based on gang affiliation or hometowns or the soccer teams they liked, whatever. Each group had its champion, which was a total joke because he was basically just the least decrepit junkie out of a whole bunch of decrepit junkies. These champions were going to try to climb this greased pole and snag the prizes for them and their buddies.

So the first guy went. His friends marched out carrying him on their shoulders and he was just a chicken-chested little kid with his hair tied back and no shirt on so you could see his skinny torso. Not very impressive, but what did I know? Maybe he was a great climber. Either way, he got a good loud cheer from the crowd. He stood there at the bottom of the pole looking up, and you could practically hear his teeth grinding, he wanted those drugs so bad. Then he jumped up as high as he could and grabbed on to the pole, and you could tell immediately that this guy was never going to make it. I mean, I don't know the first thing about climbing a greased pole, but I could tell right away that this wasn't it. He slid back down and everyone laughed at him, then he tried a few more times before the capos shooed him away. They sort of booed him off the stage, so to speak. He went back to his buddies all dejected.

The next guy came out and he was the same type: a skinny twitchy little dude with no shirt. He failed exactly like the first guy; he never got more than a few feet off the ground. Then the next one was a guy I knew. It was one of the *talacha* boys, which was what we called the cleanup boys, the kids who would do chores or run errands or that sort of thing. He did all kinds of little jobs for me; he was a good kid. One thing I felt real bad about (this was later on, well after the fiesta) was I had him tarring my roof one time after it rained, because there were big leaks in it. He was up on the roof hot-mopping it when he slipped and fell right into the boiling tar. He was burnt really badly, and I felt awful for getting him into that.

Anyway, this guy came out and right away people's hopes were raised because this kid had *equipment*. Even though he was the same scraggly, scrawny junky type, he came out with ropes, and you could see he had a plan. So we were all cheering and clapping for him. I mean, who knew at this point if his plan was any good, but at least he was thinking about it on a deeper level than the other guys. What he did was, he walked up to the base of this thing and tied a little noose at one end of each rope (there were two ropes). He stepped his feet into these nooses, then he took the other ends and tied them around the pole, basically like two more nooses, only this time around the pole.

And he started. He lifted one foot, then slid the other end of the rope as high as it would go up the pole before putting his weight on it—and it held! It slipped a little bit, but it held him. Then he lifted his other foot and slid that rope up the pole—same thing! Now we were really cheering, because this kid had potential to go all the way. Me and some of the other Tank C guys were cheering loudest of all, because we were fairly tight with this kid, so whatever he snagged off the top of the pole, we were liable to get a taste of. It was a long climb, though. It was probably twenty or thirty feet up there; it was fucking *high up*. But the kid was motivated. If you've ever been any kind of junky, any kind of serious addict, you understand what was driving this kid. He was sweating and shaking, but he stuck with it and eventually he made it all the way to the top. He picked it clean. And we were all cheering like *we'd* won something; it was a great feeling.

So this little guy grabbed all the shit and slid back down the pole where his buddies were waiting, and they mobbed him like he was a celebrity. They swarmed over him, and after they got done, he barely had anything left. He was huffing and puffing still from the effort of climbing that pole, and yet when he opened his fists he had maybe one or two papers of chiva and a couple of dollar bills. That's it; they took everything else. That's prison for you, right there in a nutshell. Poor kid.

Radio

The Great Radio Heist

THIS IS CLASSIC: ONE GUY had his own trailer that he lived in. I forget his name; American guy. Rich kid. I think he was in there for coke, maybe pot. He wasn't there for long. Anyway, he had this trailer, and he was the only guy in there who had one. It was a little silver teardrop-style trailer, like an Airstream or one of those, and he or his people had paid off the comandante and Heladio for them to look the other way so he could wheel it inside the prison and park it in the corner next to the soccer field. That was where he lived.

What was so funny about this guy is he had this *style*, this way about him where it seemed like he didn't even accept the fact that he was in prison. He acted like he was simply on vacation in Mexico; every day you'd see him laying out next to his little camper, just working on his suntan. That struck us as the craziest thing in the world, lying on the ground with your eyes closed when anything could happen, but it didn't faze him. Every day, he'd be spread out there with his drink and his big sunglasses, just lying there on his towel in the dirt imagining he was at the beach. Now, the main thing he had was this really nice stereo with an eight-track and a radio. It was a *really* nice stereo.

So one day he was laying out, he had his whole setup going, he was kicked back with his eyes shut behind these big old shades and his radio was on. He was listening to some FM rock station from San Diego. Johnny and I were sitting there not too far away and we were listening, too, and laughing about this guy, this beach bum on his great vacation. Meanwhile one of these junkies, these little vulture guys, came walking past, and he had a radio, too, only his was this dinky little handheld thing, one of the old pocket transistor deals with the antenna. Super shitty, like, two-dollar radio; you don't even see them anymore. He was grooving along, listening to his Mexican *banda* station or whatever, with the horns and all that, and it just sounded awful on this sad little radio of his. So he went past, then we saw him stop and turn around, and you could just see the wheels turning in this guy's head. He backed off a few yards and started messing with his radio. Turning the dial. I realized what he was up to and I kind of elbowed Johnny and said, "Check this out. Watch this guy here."

So we were looking and I was laughing and this little guy was *so* serious: he was turning and turning the dial, until at last he found the same station that the other guy was listening to. All of a sudden Johnny figured it out, too, and he just busted up laughing and I elbowed him again, harder this time, because I wanted to see what was gonna happen. Well, the little guy started tiptoeing over to where the other dude's radio was, and the other guy never even opened his eyes. The kid carefully set his radio—he got the volume just right—and then he carefully set this crappy little two-dollar radio down next to the other guy's fancy one, and he gently picked up the other radio and started easing the volume down on it as he was backing away. He did that for maybe four or five steps, until he was a few yards off, and then he turned and just started booking across the yard with the guy's stereo.

The beach-bum guy never moved, never even budged. I thought that was pretty clever of that little junky kid. You know he sold it for chiva the first chance he got. I love that one; I still laugh about that.

Cabra

Goat For Sale

THE WAY IT WAS SET up, there was a gap between the outer wall and the fence. The wall was cinder block, and then inside of that there was a chain-link fence, and the gap between them was maybe about twelve feet wide. In the middle there was grass, and it used to get real long, so somebody got the idea one day to get a goat and put it between the wall and the fence—you know, to eat the grass.

So they got this goat, and it was a regular-looking goat, a healthy goat, and it was doing its thing, eating the grass. It was happy there, just eating the grass. And after a while these two junkies came by, and they were looking at this goat and licking their lips; they couldn't stand it. Here these guys are starving, and there's this fat goat like two feet away from them behind this fence; it's too much. So these guys started trying to lure this goat over to the fence, and it's tough work because what did they have to offer a goat that was better than that tall grass he was chomping on? But they were determined, so even though it took a while they eventually got him over close enough so they could grab him. They grabbed hold of his leg and they started trying to drag him under the fence.

It was horrible. The poor goat was literally *screaming* the whole time while these two idiots were yanking on it, pulling and pulling and trying to haul it through this little gap where the fence was stretched out at the bottom, probably from an old escape attempt or whatever. Finally they did it, they dragged him under the fence, and he was kicking... he was kicking and screaming and they got a rope on his leg and they hung him up on the fence. Keep in mind it's not like these two guys knew what the hell they were doing— they were just a couple of amateur dumbasses trying to beat up on this poor goat. After they dragged him under and tied him up there, he was still kicking, and they started *sawing* at his neck with this dull little knife that one of them had. They were sawing away, back and forth, back and forth, and the poor goat was still screaming, and they were getting nowhere, until finally they were like, "Fuck it," and they started stabbing this goat in its neck.

A lot of people were watching by this point because this was just riveting. You know what I mean? I'm sorry, this was fascinating. It was like a nature show; you couldn't look away. So anyway, they were stabbing this poor goat, and the goat was screaming, and finally— *finally!*—they stuck it, the knife stuck in its neck. I guess they hit the artery or whatever, because blood just started spraying out of his neck. It was spraying all over the place and they were trying to catch the blood in these coffee cans. And still the goat was screaming, and now he was, like, gurgling too. I don't remember if they were going to drink the blood, or they were gonna cook with it or what, but they were definitely saving it for something. So the blood drained out of this goat and finally the goat relaxed. It just hung there, dead. They cut him down and ran off with him back to the tanks, wherever they were staying.

When they came out a little while later, they had this great big platter all piled high with goat meat. You could see they had it all laid out like they were trying to make it look nice, like in a butcher shop. They went around from place to place selling the goat meat. I remember it went pretty quickly. I never bought any directly because I didn't really cook, but I did get a couple of tacos from a guy who bought some; they were good.

It was sad what happened to that goat, sad how he died, but there was no sense wasting the meat. It was too late at that point, I believe; wasting the meat would have been even worse.

Cubeta

American Shit Bath

THERE WAS VERY LITTLE FIGHTING, I mean actual fist-fighting, in La Mesa. If someone was out of line, there were basically three main things you could do to punish them or get rid of them or humiliate them. If someone had disrespected a capo or beat him for a few dollars or something like that, that person could be greenlit for any of the three penalties. One was you could stab him, and that was intended either to kill him or just to hurt him. Another was to shoot him; that was if you wanted to kill him. And the third thing was you could give him a shit bath.

There were open sewers running through the prison like ditches, and those led out to a big cesspool, and from there they'd either pump the sewage out or treat it or something, I don't know. The way a shit bath worked was, if there was someone who needed to be taught a lesson, you'd wait until he was dressed up real nice and then you'd pay one of the little junky kids, the vultures, to take a gallon can, like a paint can, and fill it up with sewage from the ditches. They'd take this gallon can of shit and in front of everybody, they'd throw it right on the guy, and everyone would laugh, and he would be humiliated. That was how they'd keep him in check. There were always two or three shit baths on visiting days, because that's when guys would be wearing their nicest clothes.

So, to back up a little bit: I had this friend, Davy. He was from Kenosha, Wisconsin, and he was in there for smuggling pot, same as me. He lived in the carraca next door to mine in Tank C. He was a real good kid, and one thing about Davy is he was probably the prettiest male I had ever seen. I used to tell him all the time that if he would just dress up like a girl he could easily walk right out with the rest of them at the end of visiting day. He wouldn't do it, though, because he was just terrified that someone might think he was queer. How crazy is that?

Davy had a little eight-track tape player, and at night he would always play "Dark Side of the Moon" by Pink Floyd—the whole album, start to finish. He would be in his room and I'd be next door in mine and we would listen to that album until we fell asleep. We literally listened to Dark Side of the Moon almost every single night the whole time I was in there.

One day Davy asked me if he could leave his eight-track in my carraca for a little while because mine had a lock on the door and his didn't. (It wasn't much of a lock; you could

112

pick it real easy, but it was better than nothing.) So we put it in my room and went out to the yard. Before we left I told one of the talacha boys—it was actually the same kid who'd climbed the greased pole and who later on got burned real bad when he fell in the hot tar—I asked him to kind of keep an eye on my room, and I gave him a few pesos. He sat down the way a little bit watching TV and keeping one eye on my carraca. We came back a little while later and the eight-track was gone; it wasn't in my room. I asked the talacha boy who it was who'd been in my place, and he said, "It was Leon. I saw him go in your room." (The guy's name wasn't really Leon. It was something like that but I don't remember his real name, so whatever—he'll be Leon.)

Leon was an American, and he was only in there a short while, but he was a real lowlife, just a disgusting individual. He was in there for *maiming horses*. What he'd do is, he'd go down to the Agua Caliente Racetrack in Tijuana and he'd shoot a horse full of speed, to try and make it run faster than the other ones, or else he'd cut its tendon or poke it with an ice pick, you know, to slow it down. He used to sneak in there and do this kind of shit, and one day he got caught.

The kid seemed sure it was him, so I went to Leon's carraca and I said, "Man, what'd you do with the eight-track?"

He said, "What're you talking about?"

"Dude," I said, "don't fuck with me. What'd you do with the eight-track?"

"I didn't do anything with it. I didn't touch it."

"Look, I paid one of these guys to watch my door, and he saw you go in there and take the eight-track. I know you took it, now what'd you do with it?"

And he kept on denying it. So finally I said, "All right, last time I'm gonna ask you, and then there's gonna be some retribution."

And he said, "I didn't take it."

I said, "Okay," and I walked out.

Something else to know about Leon is he had this *woman*, this great big old huge fat woman with short hair, that would come in and visit him and give him money for heroin and whatever. She was so homely it was ridiculous; he was just using her to bring him money. His routine was, whenever she'd come he'd get all cleaned up and spiffy and try to look the pimp, and she thought he was the most wonderful thing in the world because he was nice to her. She'd give him whatever he asked for.

Well, I'd warned him there would be some retribution, so I let about two weeks go by and then I paid one of the runners a nickel or whatever to run up to this guy's room and tell him he had a visitor. Leon thought it was this woman, so he got himself all slicked up because he thought he was gonna get some money. About the only expensive thing he had was a real nice leather jacket, so he put that on along with a clean shirt and clean pants, then he combed his hair just so. (You know where this is going.)

114

Meanwhile, I paid another guy to get a bucket of shit. But I didn't pay him to get a one-gallon bucket of shit, I paid him to get a *five*-gallon bucket of shit. This was my friend Ron—super nice guy. We didn't want Leon recognizing who it was dumping the shit on him because, like I said, he was a pretty bad dude. He was older than us and much harder than we were, and for all we knew he could have been a murderer or anything. But Ron was getting out soon and he hated Leon too and I was paying him, so he was happy to do it. Anyway, we didn't want Leon to recognize Ron, so we put him in a disguise. We put him in a big trench coat, and he had real long hair, so we tied that up and put it up under a hat and we gave him these big old sunglasses. He looked like a spy.

So here comes Leon all slicked up in his nice jacket and his hair, and over here was Ron the spy with this five-gallon bucket of shit, and it was real heavy so he was trying not to splash it on his trench coat. I came out of the crowd behind the victim, Leon. The plan was I would distract him just long enough for Ron to get the shit on him. So I kind of disguised my voice and yelled to him. I was like, "Oh, Leon!" in this high-pitched voice. Well, he stopped and looked around, and I mean just for a few seconds, but it was perfect timing for Ron to come sneaking up behind him with the shit. I gotta hand it to Ron, he hoisted that bucket and BOOM!—he just set it perfectly right down on top of the guy's head.

You know how you see football players try to get the coach with the Gatorade at the end, and half the time they fuck it up and the guy barely gets wet, or he sees it coming? Well, Ron just set this bucket right down over this guy's head and I swear the entire yard just froze. You imagine: these guys are used to seeing these little gallon cans of shit thrown at a dude. This is a full five-gallon bucket. *Of shit*. This is basically poison.

So Leon was standing there, and of course he knew what had happened to him, but he just stood there for a second—he was probably in shock at this point—he stood there for a second, and then he just kind of tipped his head a little bit, real slow, and the bucket fell off: *CLUNK*.

Now he was standing there with everything running down him and the whole yard just exploded in laughter, and my friend Ron immediately started running back to the tanks to get out of his disguise.

I had told Ron, I said, "I won't let him catch you. If he catches you, I'll put a foot in his head or whatever I gotta do. I'm not gonna let him get you. Whatever happens, you're gonna be okay." So Ron took off while the whole yard was laughing at Leon, and I was bent over laughing, too. Then Leon broke and ran after Ron, and it turned out he was *really* fast. I mean, Ron was going top speed and he had a head start on this guy, but the guy was catching up to him. So now I took off, running after them as fast as I could, and the whole time I was thinking, "Oh no, I'm gonna have to save Ron's life." Like, "I'm gonna have to fight this crazy guy, who's covered in shit."

Ron made it through a gate, and fortunately he was smart enough to have told somebody beforehand to shut the gate as soon as he came through it. So what happened was, he just barely got through and somebody slammed the gate and then WHAM!—Leon hit the gate. I was running up right behind him at this point, so I came screeching to a halt, and he turned around so I had to try to look all casual like I'd been standing there the whole time.

He looked right at me. I looked back and said, "Wow, man, I don't know who you fucked over, but you must have really blown it this time."

He kept right on staring at me. "I know who it was," he said, "and I'm gonna get him."

I just walked away laughing. I was pretty well protected by that point, much more than he was, so I wasn't too worried about it. It was totally worth it.

The worst part of it was, he tried to clean himself up in the shower, but the shower was just this little trickle of water; it barely made it out of the wall. So it's not like you could stand under it and take a real shower. It was more like you could scoop it with your hand and keep throwing water on yourself, just tiny handfuls of water. It was hopeless.

So the word was out: no more one-gallon shit baths. From that day on, if you were gonna give somebody a shit bath, you gave them an *American* shit bath.

Tren

The Babysitter

L A MESA WAS SUPPOSED TO be a family-friendly kind of prison. There weren't a million kids, but they were around, and they lived in the tanks and the other apartments right alongside the rest of us. They were a fact of life, part of what made the place what it was, and they had to be taken care of, just like kids anywhere. At the same time, of course, you had prisoners and prison people doing what they had to do, their drugs and their conjugal visits and what have you. Sometimes the parents would need to put the kids with someone for a little while so they could deal with their business. They needed a babysitter. And just like with every other thing in La Mesa, where there was a need, someone set up a little operation, a little business, to meet it. That's how The Professor started his babysitting service.

I don't know if this guy was a real professor or not. That's what someone said he was and

119

that's what we called him. I guess he must have had some kind of university job on the outside or something, some kind of academic position. He was a smart guy, obviously, and he kind of had that bearing, you could say. He was also crazy, like a bad schizophrenic, and he struggled with that. The story I heard was that he had a good job and a family on the outside, a good life, but for some reason he just lost his mind one day. Out of nowhere he snapped and murdered his whole family. Whether that's true or not I have no idea. For all I know the guy was in there for selling dope or evading his taxes. I tend to believe it, though, because he definitely seemed like a smart, educated guy who also happened to have the potential to go nuts and slaughter his family.

Prison had been hard on The Professor; he looked like a derelict. He wore rags all the time and he seemed a lot older than he was because he had a long beard and long, greasy hair. Just a really unfortunate-looking guy. But the thing about him is he loved kids. The only thing that made him happy, that seemed to give him some peace, was being around the little kids. And he was good with them, too.

So if anybody needed some time to themselves for whatever reason, they'd bring their kids to The Professor and he'd take care of them. I think he charged something like a few pesos an hour, not much. He probably would have done it for free, but everybody has to eat. He was usually set up on the basketball court, which wasn't used all that often, for basketball, anyway; it was Mexico— they were all about soccer and baseball.

Anyway, The Professor had these plastic milk crates, and he'd put the little kids in the crates and line them up like a train and then push them all around on the slick cement. The kids loved it, and as far as I know, The Professor was never on anything but his best behavior whenever he had kids to look after. I guess the massacre was like a one-time thing.

Flauta

Goofy the Rock Star

THERE WAS A MEXICAN ROCK star named "Goofy" in there, if you can believe that. That's what they told me, anyway, that he was a famous rock star who played the flute and toured all over Mexico with Carlos Santana. Thinking about it now it seems ridiculous, and I wonder if a lot of people weren't maybe exaggerating this guy's success and popularity. It seems pretty far-fetched to be a big rock star and both have a name like "Goofy" and also play the flute. That's two strikes against you, I would think. Ian Anderson from Jethro Tull played a flute and as far as I know, that's about it for famous rock-and-roll flute players. So maybe "rock star" was overstating it a little bit.

Anyway, this guy certainly *acted* like a rock star, that's for sure. He was probably one of the biggest dipshits I encountered my whole time in La Mesa. He was a total asshole rich kid, and his mother spoiled him horribly. He was arrested for pot along with my friend Davy, who I've talked about before. They were partners in the deal and they got picked up together, but as soon as they got inside Goofy cut him loose.

Goofy lived in one of the best places in the whole prison. It was a little house near the soccer field, with a front porch and everything. His mother had bought it from Heladio. (Later on, Heladio wanted it back for some reason, and Goofy's mom came into the prison and put a stop to that right quick. I don't know if she paid him to back off, or if she threatened to make trouble for the warden or what, but she was a wealthy, connected woman. That was the only time I can think of when Heladio basically had to take no for an answer.) There was always a great big bodyguard stationed out front, and there were also beautiful girls around most days. Goofy had to have his entourage around him all the time.

He never really mingled with anybody else, unless they were rich and powerful. Whenever any bigshots were around he would come out of his little house to play his flute or otherwise make a spectacle of himself, but that was about it. Other than that, he kept to himself, just hanging out with his own little clique. He got the girls, no doubt about that, but he was one arrogant jerk. I don't care how well he played the flute.

Carne

The Cannibal

BESIDES HELADIO, THERE WERE TWO other really big-time players in there, and those were The Brothers, Robert and Johnny. They had a last name, obviously, but mostly people just called them "Robert Brother" or "Johnny Brother." Anyway, there was never any tension between them and Heladio's organization because they were basically business partners; The Brothers supplied most of Heladio's heroin. They were East L.A. guys with a big retail heroin operation back home, but in La Mesa they were strictly wholesale. They also owned a hotel and cathouse down in Puerto Vallarta. I don't know what they did to get themselves locked up, but maybe it had something to do with that. Whatever it was, they lived in La Mesa with their wives, and I think they had a pretty comfortable existence going for themselves.

Robert, the older one, lived in the women's section of the prison with his wife Helen, who was really the main day-to-day operator of The Brothers' business, as far as I could tell. I should point out that there *was* a separate area for female inmates, and it was more like what we normally think of as a prison. It was too small for anything but housing—too small for stores or restaurants or any of that kind of stuff—so by default it was basically a cellblock. The female inmates were only allowed out into the main part of La Mesa once in awhile, for visiting days and occasionally at other times. Helen could come and go as she pleased because she wasn't an inmate. She was just there to take care of Robert, and he lived in the women's section for his own safety because he was blind; I believe someone had shot him in the head, was the reason for that.

(One trippy side note about the women's prison is they had a serial killer in there, and she was just *gorgeous*. She hardly ever came out to the yard or to El Pueblito, which is what they called the business district, but when she did, the whole place would stop and stare at her because she was so beautiful, but you could tell she was just evil to her core. What she did was, she traveled all around Mexico with her old man—husband, boyfriend, I don't know—and he would hide in their hotel while she went out to the bars and nightclubs and picked up guys. She'd seduce these men and take them back to their room and then together they'd rob and murder these poor guys. I don't know if they cut up the bodies or what they did to dispose of them, but they'd cover their tracks and then move on to the next town. So they eventually got caught and the old man was sent to Tres Marías, the prison colony off the west coast of Mexico, and she was sent to La Mesa.)

Anyway, The Brothers: other than being big-time drug dealers, they were just all-around good guys, just real nice guys, and I was on good terms with both of them. I hung around with Johnny quite a bit. He was funny—he was this totally hard gangster, but every time you saw him, and I mean *every time*, he'd be wearing this white tennis getup, head to toe. White cap, white shirt, white tennis shorts. White sneakers. He always looked like he was on his way to the country club. How he kept his clothes so white I have no idea; maybe he had a bunch of identical outfits. Another thing he had was a real secure carraca. It wasn't in the corral, it was next to the fence by the front wall, right next to the infirmary. There was this long corridor with a steel door at the end of it, and Johnny had this bodyguard that was always with him, this total East L.A. badass with a shaved head and a whole bunch of tattoos. If you wanted to see Johnny, you'd knock on the steel door and then a little hatch would open up and this bodyguard would look out. You would sort of announce yourself, and the guy would close the hatch and go down the hall to see if Johnny was receiving visitors. Usually he was. I used to go over there quite a bit and just hang out with Johnny and he'd tell me stories about the prison or about his business or whatever. And sometimes we'd go for walks around the yard. On one of these walks he said he was gonna tell me who the most dangerous man in the whole prison was, the one guy I had to make sure I never got on the wrong side of. Worse than the comandante, worse than Johnny himself, worse than Heladio even. Of course I was all ears.

He pointed the guy out to me, and we were fairly far away, but he sure didn't look like much. He was just this small, sickly looking guy, real dirty, and I said, "Him?" Johnny told me again he was the most dangerous guy in the whole place. So I said, "Why's he so dangerous?" And Johnny goes,

"'Cause he's a *cannibal*, man!"

Okay, that made sense, I guess: the guy might eat you. Now of course I was fascinated by this, and I started bugging him all the time to tell me stories about The Cannibal. He said The Cannibal used to be a nobody; he was just like any other inmate. Then one day another guy was laying out getting a suntan, or else he was passed out in the yard, something like that, and for whatever reason this little dude just walked over and smashed his head with a cinder block. He just picked up a cinder block and crushed the guy's skull with it. Before they could get him off of the guy, he started pulling his brains out and eating them—*he ate the guy's brains*. That was the first time he did any cannibal stuff that they knew of. The guy spent years in the tumbas for that, literally seven or eight years in the tombs.

The conditions in there were just brutal. The way it was set up was, it was basically like dog kennels. There was this row of cages, just wire mesh cages, and they were maybe six feet deep by about four and a half, five feet tall, and just about three feet wide. Tiny cages, with a little slot to pass stuff through. And that's it.

So one day this missionary or whatever he was, this helper guy, was going through there bringing food or medicine or something, and at some point I guess The Cannibal had gotten his hands on a knife—or maybe he sharpened something that he found in there, I don't know—and this guy got too close to the cage. The Cannibal reached through the slot and grabbed hold of him and stabbed him in the stomach. He held onto this guy and stabbed him, then dropped the knife and started pulling the guy's guts out. The guy was still alive, screaming his head off, and The Cannibal just kept pulling his guts out and eating them! He was holding onto the guy and eating his guts as fast as he could.

So Johnny was telling me all these stories and I was just going, "Holy shit, this guy's terrible!" I can't even describe how bad that freaked me out. Other threats you sort of see coming, you can get out of the way or prepare or whatever. But a guy like that, he's off the charts; he's just too unpredictable.

One day I saw a few of the little vultures and they had this cannibal guy with them and they were parading him all around, trying to drum up sympathy for this guy so they could make some money off him. They were going up to visitors, and inmates, and just anybody, and they were saying, "Have some compassion for this poor guy," you know, "He's been in the tumbas for..." however many years it was. They had their arms around him like he was their best buddy, and they were collecting nickels and pesos and whatever they could get for this idiot. They put him to work like that so they could get more money for chiva. Unbelievable.

Another time I was sitting down in the sunshine, out near the fruit stand where this one killing took place, and I had my shirt off, just sitting in the sun. I had my antennas up like always, just minding my own business, but I kept an eye out for any trouble coming my way. Just making sure everything was okay, nothing was creeping on me, no one was sneaking up. I wasn't worried about it, just being cautious like I always was, not really thinking about anything in particular except my predicament, like always.

All of a sudden I felt this hand on my back, up by my shoulder blade. It was a hot day, but the hand was cold and clammy. I jumped up and spun around and I saw it was The Cannibal, and I mean, I *screamed*. I screamed at him to get the fuck away from me, and he just looked at me with the most hideous grin on his face and he laughed, like, "Heh-heh-heh-heh-heh." Fuck, it was horrible; pardon my French. He backed off like that, just "Heh-heh-heh-heh" and pointing at me like, "I'll remember you." You know that kind of look?

After that I never took my eyes off him. I was always worried about him remembering me and seeing me as a target.

Navidad

Three Wise Men

IN ANY PRISON, PEOPLE DO whatever they can to escape. In the literal sense, that means getting over, under, or through the wall.

(This is kind of a side note, but I remember once seeing a young vulture climb right over the cinderblock wall like a monkey. In broad daylight! There was nobody manning this one guard tower and the kid hauled himself over the wall right next to it and ran away. It was the craziest thing, but what happened after that was even weirder. The kid ran back across town to his mother's house and hid out there for about three days. Finally she couldn't handle him anymore and dragged him back to the prison by his ear. The problem was the kid was a stone junky and she couldn't deal with his withdrawals and all the bullshit that came along with it. She knew if he was out on the street, he'd just get himself in trouble again to support his habit, and she was too poor to give him any money herself or even much food, so she figured out, rightly I think, that he'd be better off in La Mesa than he would in her house.

That was the funniest thing, when she marched him up to the gate and made him turn himself in, like a little kid caught skipping school.)

But anyway, that's not the point of this story. The point of this story is that if people can't escape literally, you can be sure they'll try to free their *minds*. For some, that means Jesus or Allah or ~~whatever~~ the case may be. Others just go crazy, straight up. And the majority turn to drugs. A lot of them were probably into drugs before they got there, obviously; that's probably why they're there. They're predisposed to it, you could say. Others get into drugs once they're locked up, just to give themselves a little bit of relief from the boredom and the fear and the fucking despair of their situation.

The way it worked in La Mesa was drugs basically were the economy. Any cash that was present got turned into drugs so fast that they might as well have just used drugs as money. Heroin, or chiva, cocaine, grass, bennies, Mandrax—shit, probably steroids, horse tranquilizers, who knows what kind of shit they had going around. Anything you could think of. On the surface of it it was supposed to be illegal—it was definitely against the rules—but it's my belief that the rules were in place not so much to stop the drug use as they were to justify the bribes, to offer some pretext, because if you're asking a guard to look the other way on a rule violation, it's a lot more expensive if there's an actual rule being violated. If it wasn't against the rules you could just tell him to screw off. Not that you would, but you could if you wanted to. So the guards got paid, and a lot of them were pretty heavy drug users themselves, so those ones would be happy to take drugs for bribes as well.

How did the drugs get in? Different ways. Guards brought some of them in. Or visitors. Sometimes someone would just lob a package over the wall at a certain time, or they'd cut open a soccer ball and fill that up with stuff and then boot it over. With the guards, you'd pay them off and they'd drop a bundle off the catwalk into the yard as they were making their rounds. Let's say it was pot. Whoever had ordered it would take it and break it up into papers, like notebook paper basically. They'd roll it up with enough pot to make about three little joints, so you'd break that up and roll your own joints. And that was a dollar. The favorite thing was chiva, though, and most of that found its way into the prison with Heladio's girls, mostly Irma, the blonde. Nobody dared search her.

Anyway, I got it into my head pretty early on that I would like to try to move a little LSD. As far as I could tell, that was about the only drug they didn't already have on the market. It was actually Heladio that gave me the idea, indirectly. He was always on the lookout for a new high, or a different kink or whatever. And so he asked me about it fairly early into my time there. He knew I was from the States, obviously, so I guess he figured I must be up on all the latest psychedelics. Which, not to brag, but I was.

Bringing it in was easy. It was just paper, so you could put in a book, put it in your pocket, anything. They didn't even know what to look for down there at that time. I had a friend of mine bring it in to me, at first just a couple hundred hits. Not too much. Now remember, Heladio got a piece of everything, so I didn't want to fool around with that. It wouldn't be worth it to piss him off. I basically asked him for his blessing and told him I'd bring him his share of the money when I got it. But he said he wanted to try it, and he did, and he liked it, so he just kept some of the acid and told me not to worry about it. I was in business, and it was very well-received. They loved it. LSD kept me in tacos and hot dogs for a good long time in La Mesa.

Around the end of '74, my little LSD operation was really taking off. On Christmas Day, Johnny Bigotes came to see me and said he had these three farmers who wanted to try some. Pot growers, from Sinaloa, I believe. Older guys. I guess they had tried mushrooms before and liked them, so when they heard I had acid, they wanted to try that, too. All right, I said, bring them over.

I should probably say a little bit about Christmas in prison. It sucked; of course it did. But one of the things that made La Mesa more tolerable than regular prisons at that time of year was the way it felt more like a real community, like an actual small town because of all the different people who lived there, the kids especially. That helped with holidays, because everybody relaxed a little bit and tried to be happy, and it was more convincing because it wasn't just a bunch of angry dudes in cells with bars on them. They also let us stay out late on Christmas.

So it was late at night and I was walking around the yard. I was on psychedelics myself, tripping out on the lights and the Christmas music and stuff, feeling pretty good. But then I got to thinking, and if you've ever dropped acid or anything like that, you know how easy it is to just fall into a line of thinking, like a train of thought you get on and you can't get off. I was looking around and I kind of stepped outside of myself for a second and started thinking, "Shit, look where I am. I'm spending Christmas in prison! In Mexico! How the hell am I even dealing with this right now?" You know, like that. Like: "Jesus Christ, this is terrible! I must be nuts not to be just completely freaking out right now!"

I started feeling sorry for myself then, and I thought it might not have been the smartest idea I ever had to drop this shit on Christmas. My trip was turning bad; I was on a bummer a little bit. So I started back toward my carraca to kind of hole up and deal with myself when Johnny hollered to me and came walking over with the three little farmers. They had their big old hats on and their cowboy shirts and their boots. And they had their money with them, they were ready to go, so I turned them on right there in the yard; I gave them the acid and showed them how to put it on their tongues. Then while they were waiting for it to kick in, I took off back to my place because now it was really turning ugly for me. I was feeling all trapped and sad and sorry for myself.

I hightailed it back to the tank, and by now my imagination was just going crazy on me. It was like an oven in the tank with the bodies all piled on top of each other and I had to step over everybody to get to the stairs. Out of nowhere my mind started telling me that everyone was dead, that it was corpses piled all over the place. It was just horrible. So I got back to my carraca and I locked the door and curled up with the pillow over my head, totally regretting the trip and just waiting for it to be over, praying for it. Then all of a sudden I thought, "Oh shit—what if those guys are having a bad trip, too? What am I gonna do if they have a bad trip and decide they're gonna come and lynch me?" Or shoot me or stab me or whatever. I started getting all these paranoid thoughts. This went on for probably a couple of hours. And right in the middle of this total panic attack, I heard a little tap at my door; I heard someone come up the stairs real quiet, and then there was this little tap at the door. Damn it.

Of course I thought, "Well, this is it. I'm gonna die now." I was sure of it. And I didn't even fight it. It just made sense to me at that point, in that condition. Why *wouldn't* I die? So I walked over and opened the door, and there were these three little old farmers standing there. Their eyes were all huge and they were glowing like some kind of Christmas miracle, like they had halos around them. Just grinning ear to ear. They stared at me, smiling, for the longest time and then they stuck out their hands and said,

"*Más.*"

That's it: just the one word, and these smiles. That just about made my year.

Mártir

Hank the Fallen Hero

I FIRST MET HANK IN lockup at La Ocho. He was the Marine who'd taken the fall for his buddies after they all got caught smuggling pot around the fence down there at the shoreline. It was Hank's example that gave me the idea to spring my own partners the same way. Hank was a really good guy, just a standup character, and he looked like Captain America.

Anyway, we both wound up in La Mesa. Hank did all right for himself, I'd have to say, even though he'd never been to prison before and he looked even whiter than me. Everyone sensed that he was an honorable dude, and even if he wasn't the hardest guy in there, you had to respect that, which people did. At first his buddies, the ones he took the fall for, they would come around and visit him and bring him money or food or whatever, but one by one they stopped coming. They abandoned him. And his parents, back there on the farm or wherever, I think they just wrote him off as a junky and a criminal. They were aware of his situation, but they didn't care. He didn't talk about them much except to say that they didn't want to have anything to do with him.

But I would say probably the worst thing that happened to Hank was he befriended this one particular Mexican guy. His nickname was "Borrego," same as mine, but he had black curly hair instead of blond. Borrego turned Hank on to some chiva, and that's when Hank caught hepatitis.

There are, I believe, three different kinds of hepatitis, and a whole bunch of ways you can get it. For some people it's no big deal and for others it's deadly. Well, when Hank got it, he just became horribly sick right off the bat. It's always been my belief that he got it from the needle. That's just a feeling, but for some reason I've always been sure that was what did it. Anyway, it just laid him out. He went crazy from it. Here he was, this nice, levelheaded kid, and within a couple days he's sick as a dog and just raving. I went to see him in his carraca one day—this was before I knew what he had—and I knocked on the door, and on the other side I heard him holler, "Fuck off! Get out of here and leave me alone!" We were good buddies, so I was thinking he must not have known it was me. So I knocked again, and I told him who it was. Again he said, "Get the fuck out of here!" Like I said, at this point I didn't know how sick he was, so I was just like, "All right, fuck that guy." And I left.

Well, the next day this Borrego character, the one who'd shot him up, came up to me and told me that Hank was real, real sick, and that they were gonna take him over to the infirmary. I hurried over to his place—he was the only American in E Tank—I hurried over and saw that some of the inmates from the tank had him on a stretcher. They all had bandanas tied over their faces like bandidos because they thought he had the plague or something, literally. They wanted him out of there. He was rolling around on the stretcher and the sweat was just pouring out of him and there was puke all over his cheek and his eyes were rolled up in his head and they were all yellow. He really looked terrible; a big strong Marine and he looked like he was dying.

They ran him over to the infirmary and basically dumped him there. Well, the medic at the infirmary was no braver than these guys; he didn't want to get close to him, so Hank was getting no medical care whatsoever. I didn't know what the hell to do for him, so I tried the only thing I could think of, which was to call this woman I knew on the outside and put her on the case to try to get the Marines involved. Or the Navy, or whoever was in charge of all that. And God bless her, she ran with it, she called all over the place, putting pressure on people. At first they didn't want anything to do with it. They said he's a junky and he's a smuggler and like this, and there was nothing they could do for him. Well, she just kept calling and calling and hammering away at them, telling them "Look, this kid is real sick in there and they won't help him, so if you guys don't send a doctor or somebody down to take care of him, he's gonna die!" Finally she told them that if

Hank died, she was gonna call all the newspapers and the TV stations and tell them that the Navy had left this guy down there to croak when they could have saved him. That finally got through to them.

This had been going on for a few days already when they finally agreed to send a doctor down from Camp Pendleton. When the doctor showed up, it was me and Johnny Bigotes taking care of Hank in the infirmary because no one else would touch him, and Hank was bare-ass naked because he was just sweating and burning up. This doctor came in and took one look at Hank and jabbed an I.V. into him, hooked up to this bag of fluid, saline fluid or something. He gave me and Johnny the dirtiest look, like we were two pieces of shit, as if we'd caused Hank to be like this instead of being the only ones doing fuck-all to help the poor guy. The doctor told us if we couldn't keep the fluid in him that Hank was gonna die for sure. His liver was shutting down. I said I'd do my best, but ▓▓▓▓▓, the kid was in convulsions, he was thrashing all over while I tried to keep the needle in him. As fast as the fluid was going into him he was pissing it out, literally pissing all over the place and sweating like crazy. We could see him drying out right in front of our eyes. His lips were cracking right in front of us. We tried to hold him down but he was completely delirious, thrashing all around.

Then the doctor was gone. We stayed with Hank most of the night like that and he wasn't getting any better, so finally the Mexicans, the infirmary workers, came in and said they were gonna take him over to the hospital because it looked like he was pretty close to dying, like this was the end. They wheeled him out and put him in an ambulance for the ride to the hospital, and he died along the way.

That just broke my heart. Here was this real good kid, this honorable kid, and everyone just abandoned him. He didn't deserve that. He especially didn't deserve to die that way, not in that place. So I decided I would reach out to his family, try to tell them what kind of a man their son turned out to be. How he took the fall for his buddies and what a brave thing that was. I would want to know that if it was my kid in that situation. So I wrote them a long letter, and I had my friend, the woman who'd pestered the Navy, track down his parents in Kansas and mail it to them. And I never heard a thing back from them. I don't know if it did any good or not, or if they'd just written him off and that was the end of it.

Paredón

Guards Are Prisoners, Too

I'VE ALWAYS BELIEVED IT'S IMPORTANT—and just plain smart, frankly—to treat people with respect until they disrespect you. It makes life easier, and since no one can see the future, you never know when it's going to pay off. Situations can change suddenly; you can find yourself at the mercy of the guy who was maybe lower than you in the pecking order the day before, and then you're gonna be happy you weren't a dick to him for no reason. Or you'll be sorry if you were. Some of the guards were like that, just regular people doing their jobs and not going out of their way to make life hard for us prisoners. Others—and you see this a lot in positions of authority—others got off on the power they had over us, and they never passed up a chance to lock us up or pistol whip us or just generally push us around. And sometimes it came back to haunt them.

Compared to most jobs, being a guard at La Mesa was pretty shitty. The wages were low and the danger level was high, both in terms of the violent situations they were always getting involved in but also from the constant threat of disease with all the hepatitis and dysentery and tuberculosis and everything else that was constantly going around. It was a hazardous job that did not pay well. Morale sucked, too. They didn't get much in the way of training from the powers-that-be that ran the place, and it would be an understatement to say they were poorly equipped. They were a sad sight. They had uniforms, but they were ragged and outdated. I think they were left over from the '40s, or maybe the early '50s. Only a few of the guards had hats, which they had to provide themselves. They went for those high peaked motorcycle caps like the one Marlon Brando wore in "The Wild One." I believe they were responsible for their own firearms as well, which is just crazy. So you had all these guards with mismatched weapons: some of them had decent hunting rifles, some had cheap Saturday Night Special-type handguns that were liable to blow up if they ever had to fire them, and a few had Wild West-style pistolas, old-school Colt revolvers in leather gun belts with the bullets all around. Those looked sweet; I don't know how well they worked, but they sure looked cool. On the whole, though, the inmates had better guns than the guards. It was a sorry-ass operation, no two ways about it.

There was one funny thing that happened most nights after lockdown. Just to set the scene, there were gun towers every hundred feet or so along the top of the wall, with a catwalk connecting them. After I had my carraca dialed in all nice, with my bed up in the loft under the window, I was able to lie there and look out at the stars, and that was great, but it meant that my bed was right next to the catwalk. From time to time during the night the guards were supposed to holler at one another, sort of working their way from one tower to the next, so everyone could make sure everyone else was where they were supposed to be. The towers had numbers, and the way it worked was the guy in Tower One would yell out, *"Uno alerta!"* And then the guy in Tower Two would yell,

"Dos-e alerta!"

And the next one would go, *"Tres-e alerta!"*

Then *"Cuatro alerta!"* You get the idea.

They were supposed to do this every hour or so, but occasionally a guy would fall asleep, and then it would be like, "Dos-e alerta!" And he would wait. Then he'd go again: "Dos-e alerta!" Then louder: "DOS-E ALERTA!" And then you'd hear the door open and these footsteps running down the catwalk, and then he'd pound on the door and the other guy would be like, ▓▓▓▓▓▓▓▓▓!" and then he'd yell, "Tres-e alerta!" and they'd go from there. Goofy-ass guards. It was funny.

But overall, as I said, it was a pretty unrewarding life, being a guard at La Mesa, so I guess it was understandable that a high percentage of the guards would supplement their income with various kinds of illegal shit. Not all of them, but a lot of them would try to steal whatever valuables they could get their hands on from the lower-ranking prisoners. Not the top guys, obviously, like Heladio or The Brothers—those guys were pretty much untouchable. But the rest of us had to watch out. More than once I caught a guard at night trying to fish through my window the same way the trusties in La Ocho had done, with a coat-hanger hook on the end of a long pole. I don't know what they thought they were going to get off of me—it's not like I had anything worthwhile—but it pissed me off nonetheless. The thieving was nickel-and-dime stuff, though; the real corruption was all about drugs.

Most of the drugs came into the prison through visitors, or through the girls that Heladio and his crew brought in, but a big part of the drug supply was smuggled in by the guards themselves. Heladio or The Brothers would have their people on the outside pay off the guard on the outside and give him the stuff to bring in. Then at a certain time in a certain spot, the guard would just walk along the catwalk and drop the package into the yard. That was it. There'd be some guys waiting for it and they'd bring it back to the capo's place to split it into smaller packages for resale. Easy. Sometimes the guards would get paid in cash, sometimes in drugs—a lot of them were hooked on chiva just like the prisoners.

But even in a place as corrupt and out of control as La Mesa, there's still a chance that sooner or later the crooked shit will catch up with the people doing it. Maybe a guard was so strung out he wasn't pulling his weight, or maybe he'd done something to piss off the federales, but from time to time one of these guys would be targeted for surveillance or an investigation and then it was just a matter of time until he wound up in the prison right along with the rest of us. The federales pretty much always got what they wanted, so if they decided a guard needed to go to prison, that guy was going, no question.

(The feds were total pricks, pricks and bullies. Their jurisdiction covered the whole country, as their name would suggest, so they could come in and push everyone around whenever they wanted. They certainly were not shy about using their authority. One of the worst things they did, and they did it all the time just because they enjoyed it, was the way they used to herd guys around. The federales had these automatic rifles, and what they would do is, when they wanted a bunch of us to go somewhere, they'd just squeeze off a burst of gunfire out of these things, just spray a line of bullets in the dirt, and everyone would run from it. Then they'd do it again on the other side, and we'd all run back. That way they could just sweep whole groups of guys wherever they wanted them to go, because nobody wanted to get hit with these damn machine guns.)

Anyway, as if all of that weren't bad enough, for a lot of years, including the time that I was there, they had a rule in La Mesa that said if you were a guard and somebody escaped on your watch, you had to serve out the rest of his term yourself. Think about how fucked up that is; that's a true story. So for all these various reasons, every once in a while you'd have a guard thrown in with the prisoners. Now, this was not the same situation you'd picture from American prisons or American prison shows or whatever. There definitely was no such thing as segregated units for former law-enforcement or anything like that; it was strictly Gen Pop. But the guards wouldn't necessarily be singled out for any kind of rough treatment. Everyone recognized that they were just guys like us, sad sacks with shitty jobs, and they were pretty much treated the same as everybody else.

If the guy in question had gone out of his way to be an asshole or a bully, though, and then wound up inside as a prisoner, he got it bad. They'd make sure he got a shit bath right off the bat, or else they'd stab him or beat him up or take his stuff—depends on what he'd done to them. But as I've said before, if you've been a jerk to people for no good reason, you can't exactly cry about it when they want to get you back. How a guy wouldn't expect that to happen, I have no idea.

Travestí

Robbie Was A
Ladies' Man

I HAVE A YOUNGER BROTHER, Robbie, and he was about eighteen or nineteen at the time I was in La Mesa. One day he came down to visit me. Robbie was a real good-looking kid: long hair, quite the ladies' man. All the girls liked Robbie. I knew he was coming, so I made sure to meet him up by the front so he wouldn't have to walk through the prison by himself looking for me. So I met up with him by the gate and we walked back to my carraca. Robbie was strutting through the place like a superstar, checking everything out.

We walked through the yard, through the corral, and we entered C Tank. Robbie had never seen anything like it; he was looking everywhere just trying to take it all in. Anyway, I didn't see this, but as I led him up the stairs to my carraca, he was busy checking out this hot chick that he saw. When we got inside my place, Robbie said, "Damn, Steve, who was that girl out there? She was checkin' me out!"

It was still morning, so I was kind of bumfungled I guess you could say, because there weren't usually any hot girls around that early in the day. The real cute ones usually started coming in in the early afternoon. I was confused. So I asked him, "Where did you see her?"

He said, "Right out there. She was watching TV."

I went and poked my head out, looked down the row to where the television was, and there was this transvestite sitting there. A young dude, maybe seventeen, eighteen years old, all done up and smiling at me. Not bad for a transvestite, honestly, but it was definitely a guy. I closed the door and turned back to Robbie. I said, "Robbie, you know that wasn't no chick, right? That's a dude."

And Robbie said, "No way."

I tried to explain it to him, how there were all these transvestites in there, these men who like to dress up like women, and you had to be careful so you didn't get fooled. He was my brother; I was trying to look out for him, but he just kept shaking his head. He didn't believe me. He got up like he was gonna go take another look and I stood in his way, tried to stop him before he opened the door again. "Please don't open the door," I said. "If you look out there again, she's just gonna come

152

down here and then we'll never get rid of her."

But Robbie was just certain it was a girl. He couldn't stand to think he'd just been flirting with a guy, so he sort of pushed past me and opened the door. Sure enough, the transvestite was still there. She smiled over at Robbie and he squinted back at her like he was really studying her, trying to figure out if she was a chick or a dude. Then she got up and started walking over, so Robbie slammed the door shut and went into a full-on panic. He was like,

"Shit, man, I think it's a *guy*! He's coming over here! What are we gonna do?!"

"Yeah, no shit!" I said, and I was kind of annoyed with him now because that's exactly what I'd just told him was going to happen. I was happy to see my brother, but why did he have to go and bring this crazy transvestite into the scene? So I said, "I don't know what *you're* gonna do, Robbie. It's your girlfriend. I wasn't the one told you to flirt with her."

Sure enough, there she was, knocking on the door. She knocked and knocked while Robbie and I argued over who was going to have to go and deal with her. Finally I just said "Fuck it," and I went and opened the door. There was this guy—it was very obviously a guy when you saw him from that close up—there's this guy, and he's smiling all big and trying to look past me into the room. You know, looking for Robbie. I tried to be nice, tried to close the door without being rude about it, saying, "No, no thank you, we're fine, no thank you, there's been a mistake, goodbye," that kind of stuff. The transvestite got all huffy and marched off, cussing me out the whole way.

So Robbie and I hung out for a while in my carraca until the coast was clear, then we snuck out of there and went to grab a hot dog. Robbie kept his head down as we walked through the prison. No more strutting and flirting for him, not until he was safely back home. He'd learned his lesson.

Enchufe

The Flames of Passion

HOLY SHIT, THIS ONE WAS terrifying. It started out so awesome and ended up with me just about crapping my pants I was so scared, except I wasn't wearing any pants.

All right, what happened was, I was up in my carraca with this chick. Super hot. She and her boyfriend had come down to visit my friend Davy, but the boyfriend was a stone junky and whenever they came down the first thing he'd do is go and score some chiva. He'd shoot that and then he'd nod out and she'd be all horny and frustrated and stuck with this unconscious boyfriend. So I'm a generous guy, I'm gonna take care of her; I wouldn't leave her like that. It was risky, though, because the boyfriend was a bad, bad dude— this guy was terrible.

He and a buddy of his had both gone off to Vietnam and did at least a couple tours there, maybe more. Both of them came back with pretty serious drug habits and severe mental problems. They ended up in San Diego where they were doing all sorts of really bad shit: robbing banks, robbing gun stores—crazy, violent shit. They used to come down and visit Davy because they had this plan where they wanted to find a connection in Mexico so they could trade a bunch of these stolen guns for a great big shitload of pot. And whenever they came down they always brought their girlfriends with them, who were both super hot and just freaky as all hell. One was a blonde and the other one was a brunette; it's the blonde one I'm talking about in this story.

Anyway, so the boyfriend was a violent psycho and he was out cold in Davy's carraca while me and the girl were going at it in my place next door.

Before I go on, I gotta explain a little bit about how the electrical system worked inside the carracas—you'll see why in a minute. There were two wires, a ground wire and a hot wire, running through the whole place, and in each carraca there were two leads that came off of them. That was how you could tap in to the electrical supply: you'd take whatever appliance you wanted to use and just touch the wires to the prongs of the plug. For example, say you had a light bulb. You'd touch the ground wire to the base of the bulb, then you'd touch the hot wire to the base, too, and it would light up. There was your light. In my carraca I had a little hot plate type of thing, which was basically just this thick coiled wire that looped around and around and got hot. I don't know what you call it in English but down there they called it a *resistencia*, so it was some sort of a resistor, I guess. These things were always burning out but they were real handy and they only cost about two bucks or so, so those were pretty popular. You could lay tortillas across them and cook the tortillas, or you could heat up soup or whatever you wanted with it. I had scrounged up a couple of old cooking pots somewhere, which came in handy for heating beans or stew or whatever I had.

(As I've said before, the federales gave me about seven bucks every two weeks to buy food, but I generally blew through that far too quickly to actually live on it for the whole two weeks. Meanwhile the state prisoners, which was most of the population of La Mesa, got a decent sized helping of beans or some kind of stew most nights. My buddy Johnny Bigotes, who was a state prisoner, was a skinny little guy who never ate much anyway, plus he was just a generous person, so thank God he didn't mind sharing with me. He'd come back with the food and we'd pick the bugs out of it and heat it up on my resistencia, which we also used to make coffee. Not real coffee, but a fake version that we made out of what they called "coffee rinds." Not grinds, or grounds—rinds. It wasn't actual coffee beans, but it was the branches of the coffee bushes. You could boil those for a really long time and make coffee. I would buy some canned milk and put a little bit of that in with the coffee, and that was our special treat. We'd cook the same branches over and over until the coffee came out clear, and that's when we knew it was time to get more rinds.) Anyway, the point of all that is there were these two leads hanging down from the main line, which ran from carraca to carraca up near the roof line. That was how you got electricity into your carraca.

So I had been flirting with this blonde since I first saw her and now that her boyfriend was nodded out, she'd come knocking on my door. So we were in my place going at it, and it was amazing. I was behind her, standing up, and she was flailing all around and backing up into me. I guess she pushed me backwards closer and closer to the wall until eventually I bumped into the wires, or brushed against them or something. I didn't notice it at first because I was so into what we were doing, but I guess the bare ends of the wires touched each other and shorted out. By the time I turned around and saw what was going on, the wires were on fire. Electricity was arcing between them, crackling back and forth, and the fire was climbing up toward the ceiling, toward the main line. I was like, "Holy shit! This whole place is gonna burn down!"

So now this chick and I were standing there buck naked, neither of us knowing what to do, with little fires breaking out all along the path of these wires. The paisley tapestry was on fire, and the cardboard wall a little bit, and I honestly don't think I've ever been so scared in my whole life; this was the worst, because the whole place was like kindling. ~~Jesus Christ,~~ just think what this places was made of! It was all dried-out old wood and cardboard and cloth, and we were all stacked

158

on top of each other and locked inside. The stampede alone would kill pretty much everyone as soon as they figured out what's going on and really started to panic.

So the girl started putting on her clothes, and at first I was putting on my clothes, too, because what else could I do? And then I was like, "Fuck it," because this was way more serious than getting busted naked with this psycho's girlfriend.

By now the fire had climbed up to the main line and was working its way over into the next carraca, not Davy's place but the other one. I ran over there and banged on the door, but those guys were already wide awake and yelling. So I went to the next one, and I banged on their door, and I figured the fire hadn't reached that place yet because the guy inside was all groggy as if I'd woken him up. But somehow he was able to stop the spread of it; somehow he knew how to cut the power or whatever he did to stop it. So the fire was put out without terrorizing everybody and without causing a riot in the tank.

What it did do, however, was knock out the electricity in the whole tank for a day or two and cause a fair amount of fire damage to the neighbors' place. The tank capo and the guys whose stuff was damaged and the amateur electrician who was gonna fix the wiring all got together to figure out how much money I owed them for the trouble I'd caused. It ended up being three or four bucks for some wire and for the guy's time to fix it, and a few more dollars to get the neighbors a new hot plate and lamp. They went pretty easy on me;

mostly I think we were all just glad the whole place didn't go up in flames.

I was a lot more careful after that—with the electrical stuff, anyway. I still pushed my luck with that dude's girlfriend every chance I got.

Permanente

A Star Is Born

NO MATTER WHAT KIND OF industry or business you're talking about, when there's a lot money at stake there's bound to be competition for it. That's just the way the world works. Well, I think I've made it clear there was a ton of money changing hands around the prison. To be in charge of that would put you in a pretty lucrative position to say the least. If you were in that spot you'd have to expect there'd be guys looking to take you down.

When I showed up, the head of the whole place was Heladio Diaz, no question. Heladio was The Godfather. He had his bodyguards and his underlings and what have you, but at that time I don't think he really faced any serious challengers. The average prisoner didn't care who was in charge as long as the drugs kept flowing and the guards were taken care of and the violence never got too far out of hand. We were happy with Heladio, and I think he knew it; he seemed pretty relaxed most of the times I saw him.

Where things got shaky is when the drug supply dried up, the heroin supply in particular, which it did from time to time. Maybe there was a big bust on the outside, a big drug seizure; that could dry up supplies everywhere for a while because the dealers either didn't have it any more or they were keeping their heads down because they were scared they'd get busted too. In Mexican prisons, at that time at least, the last thing the authorities wanted was to choke off the flow of drugs. They had certain ones they didn't like and didn't want in there, like Mandrax for example. Mandrax is a downer, but it can make you violent if you eat too much of it, so they didn't want that. They didn't like alcohol for the same reason, but there's no way to stop it, not when you can make your own so easily. The two they really didn't mind were pot and heroin, because pot makes you mellow and heroin makes you happy and usually makes you just want to sit down. If you were running a prison and you had your choice between dealing with a bunch of angry, sober criminals or mellow, nodded-out junkies, you'd probably let the dope slide, too. You'd look the other way. I would.

And like I said, the only time things really got sketchy is when the heroin wasn't getting through. At first the price would go up, and then guys would get desperate, and the vultures would start robbing each other for it. The whole mood would get dark; everybody would be depressed, and they'd start looking for other things they could do, like sniffing glue, drinking more, eating more Mandrax— all recipes for violence. Stabbings would increase; the place would start feeling like a powder keg. Like you could hear the fuse burning down: *hisssssss*. Fuck, it was scary sometimes.

And then always, right before it got totally out of control, like magic the taste would come back, the heroin, and everyone would relax.

Here's the thing, though: the only loyalty a junky has is to whoever gets him his shit, and that's only as long as he's getting it. So if you did want to make a play for control of the prison, those dry spells were the opportunity. If you could supply the chiva when Heladio was dry, you could make a serious claim on his business. You could establish yourself. And that's what this one young guy did.

"Estrella" was his name, which means "star," and did he ever act like it. Remember I said before how Johnny Brother was always slicked up in his white tennis outfit? Well, Johnny Brother had nothing on Estrella. This kid favored white also, but with him it was white track suits, like Adidas track suits, and he had these gold chains he would wear, always on the outside of his jacket where everyone could see them. Permed hair—he was a total dick.

But he hustled hard. He got his hands on some heroin when even Heladio couldn't, and he made his mark. There was one dry spell, just awful, I want to say it was almost close to a week, and the place was ready to blow, like full-on riot time, when Estrella came up with the chiva. It was like the hallelujah angels singing down on this kid. Everybody got high, and everyone was so grateful to Estrella. He kicked Heladio down his ten percent just like he was supposed to. Made a big show of it, marching to his place with cash in a briefcase, and Heladio, even though he felt punked by this kid upstaging him like that, he had to bite his lip and take it.

Soon after that Heladio got his supply up and running again and Estrella dropped back, sort of faded into the background, but he was on the map now. He was just this scrub from B Tank, just a glorified vulture himself, really, but for a brief moment he'd established himself as a player.

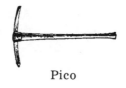

Pico

Tunnel to Nowhere

I MENTIONED BEFORE HOW I used to go and visit with Johnny Brother quite a bit. Robert too, a little, but mostly Johnny. He and I became pretty good friends. Johnny's carraca, as I said, was across from the infirmary. Well, on the other side of that was the cesspool. It was this big tank, almost like a pond, and it was covered up with a big wooden lid like a platform, but only partially. So you'd think it would stink to high heaven but it really didn't. Even on super-hot days it never stank too bad, and I don't really understand the engineering behind stuff like that but I guess it had something to do with the water on top, like somehow they'd figured out how to make all the shit and sludge and stuff sink to the bottom and then the layer of water would keep the smell from escaping; I really don't know.

But anyway, this other buddy of mine, a guy named Alex, lived in the carraca next door to mine with my friend Davy. Alex and his wife were both hairdressers, and they had gotten caught selling heroin out of their hair salon, so that's how Alex wound up in the prison. From the day he arrived, he was dead set on getting out of there. You couldn't hold this guy; he was totally determined to escape. He was so committed to it that other people started believing he might really pull it off, so they began paying him money to bring them along, too. The plan he'd worked out was to dig a tunnel under the wall and get out that way. Pretty straightforward.

Not long before we got there, a bunch of other inmates, mostly Americans, had tunneled out and escaped, which was why they now tried to make sure all the Americans stayed in the corral, because it was more secure and farther from the outside wall. The way those earlier guys had done it is they dug down through the floor in a corner carraca, in the strip of apartments along the fence by the front wall. They did it with the cooperation of Johnny and Heladio, who brought in a little storage shed for them to hide the dirt in, the dirt they'd dug out of the hole. Well, when that one went down, the comandante and everyone had been pretty embarrassed, so they made a big show of throwing Johnny in the tumbas in order to show that no one was above the law (no one but Heladio, I guess). It was strictly for show, of course—I don't think Johnny even spent one full day in the hole. They probably snuck him back out to his place after lockdown.

Alex had the idea that he was gonna do it the same way, with one notable improvement that actually came from me. One of the problems with the earlier escape was that they hadn't figured out a plan for what to do once they came up out of the ground outside the prison; they just broke and scattered, with the guards shooting at them and everything. So I had the idea to get some accomplices on the outside pull up right next to the wall with an unmarked van, like a small panel truck. And there would be a hole cut in the floor of the van just big enough for a person to crawl through. The van would park right on the spot where the guys were gonna surface, and they'd come up out of the ground and crawl right inside of the getaway vehicle, and nobody could see shit unless they were lying on their bellies looking under the van. Once the van drove away and the guards got around to noticing the hole in the ground, everyone would be long gone.

So that was my awesome contribution, and for that idea Alex let me come along for free, not that I thought it would work. Still, I was glad to be invited, because a lot of people weren't. Some guys were excluded because they were almost done with their sentences anyway, so it wasn't worth the risk; others were thought to have loose lips, so they couldn't be trusted; and some weren't allowed in on it for the simple reason that nobody liked them.

The reason I thought it wasn't going to work, and I tried to tell them this, was that they were being completely stupid about where they were putting the dirt. Obviously they didn't want to run the storage shed play again—the comandante would spot that a mile away after the last time. So I said they should take an empty carraca and put it in there. No guards ever went into the tanks anyway, so there was no reason anyone would ever have to find out, but I think Alex was too cheap to rent another carraca to stash the dirt, or maybe he was just too stubborn to listen to me.

The hole they were digging started inside of a tiny carraca Alex had rented right next door to Johnny Brother's place out by the front of the prison. From there they were going to head under the fence and beneath the grassy buffer zone leading out to the wall. The total distance was probably something like ten or twelve yards; this was a sizeable amount of dirt we're talking about. The part that was so dumb about it is they were dumping all that dirt into the cesspool. Every night, they would haul it around the end of the building and dump it in the cesspool. Stupid. When you walked by in the daytime you could see the water level getting higher and higher and higher. I tried telling them that they were gonna fuck up whatever system was in place for clearing out that sewage sludge, but they didn't listen to me.

Needless to say, it wasn't long before my prediction came true and these geniuses clogged up the sewer system until the cesspool backed up and spilled over the side. It stunk pretty bad then, that's for sure. Until it flooded, the authorities had no idea what was going on, but as soon as that sewage stink started filling up the administration building, the comandante's office especially, by God they were gonna get to the bottom of it. It didn't take them long to come knocking at

Johnny's door and the door next to his, where the digging was going on, and that's when the whole thing fell apart. All those guys got busted. Johnny got away with it because he had the deep pockets to get away with pretty much anything, but Alex and the others ended up in the tumbas. I hadn't contributed anything but my big getaway idea, and the guys kept their mouths shut about that, so I skated free.

Sinfonola

Rock and Roll
Will Set You Free

O NE OF THE MOST POPULAR places to eat in La Mesa was this little hamburger spot that was headed up by a guy I knew. He was a real nice guy, a great soccer and baseball player. He was in there for murder, but it was self-defense; he really was a good guy. Anyway, he and his buddy started this place and the reason everyone liked it is it felt like an actual little restaurant in there. It was a tiny spot, just a few tables, but the chairs matched, and they had it decorated real nice, like an old '50s diner. On one wall they had an old-style Wurlitzer jukebox with the colored lights and the bubbles going up the sides. The records in it were out of date, but that just added to the old-timey vibe of the place. It really felt like you were going back to a simpler time when you walked in there. You could almost tell yourself that you

171

weren't in prison anymore, at least for a little while. I forget what they called it, but it was a great place.

One day this American named Fred, who was in there for smuggling weed oil, went down to the hamburger place with a big pile of money and talked these guys into selling him their jukebox. He just kept upping his offer until they couldn't say no; it was that much cash. They sold him the jukebox, but even as they were doing it they wondered why anyone would want to buy it. Why not just come down to the burger shop and visit it? Just put your nickel in it like everyone else, if you love it so much. It didn't make any sense. But when Fred told them his idea for the jukebox, they got it. It was a brilliant plan.

What Fred had done was have his wife and another friend on the outside find a shop in Tijuana that specialized in repairing old jukeboxes, and they arranged for the guys from the shop to come and pick up the jukebox to haul it back to their place to be fixed. Now, the jukebox was already in perfect working order, but that was before Fred opened up the back of it and yanked all the guts out. He hollowed it out until it was basically an empty cabinet, except if you looked at it from the front, through the glass, it looked like a normal jukebox. Then Fred, who was not a small guy—he was actually a big weightlifter, musclebuilder-type of guy—squeezed himself into the back of the jukebox and they closed the door on him. When the repair guys came to pick up the jukebox, they wheeled it out on a big appliance dolly and hoisted it up onto their truck. The guards were watching them the whole time, but they wheeled Fred out right under their noses.

As soon as they got it back to their shop and opened it up, Fred jumped out and took off. The repair guys must have nearly died of shock! Craziest damn thing—I wish I'd thought of that.

Televisión

Steve the TV Star

I HAD SEEN HIM AROUND here and there, but the one and only time I ever had any personal dealings with the comandante happened one day when I was sitting on a bench with my shirt off smoking a joint with Johnny Bigotes. We were just chilling there, smoking some pot in the sunshine, when we looked up and saw the comandante heading right for us with Heladio Diaz and a TV news crew. So Johnny and I were like, "Holy shit," okay? Obviously.

The regular guards, your run-of-the-mill guards, they didn't give two shits if you smoked a joint; if anything, that made their job easier. But the comandante had to keep up appearances, especially with a camera in the mix. I recognized the reporter. It was a guy called Roberto Salinas who was a big-time TV news reporter at Channel 8 in San Diego. This was back when there were only three channels, so that was a pretty big deal.

It was him, a cameraman and the comandante, and then trailing behind them was Heladio. Heladio had this look on his face like, "*Ix-nay on the ope-day*, assholes!" He was shaking his head at us. I forget which one of us was holding the joint at that exact moment, but we put it behind our backs and then there was this comical little moment where we were passing it back and forth to each other behind the bench, trying to make the other guy hold the damn thing. Finally we got it put out, sort of smushed it out on the back of the bench and then I think we dropped it there, trying to be all casual about it. So we got rid of the joint, but I was already high off my ass when they came walking over to talk to us.

The comandante walked up and started talking to me in real broken English, saying this guy here wants to interview you. So Roberto Salinas stepped up and introduced himself and shook my hand. He seemed like the perfect newscaster, all smooth and put-together. I told him my first name only and asked him what he wanted with me. He said he was doing a series of reports about Americans locked up in Mexico; I believe that was the point of it. He said he wanted to ask me some questions about why I was there, how they were treating me, what the prison was like, that kind of stuff. I said, "No way." I didn't want to talk to this guy. What was I supposed to say? It's prison; it sucks.

So I told him there were a lot of other Americans in there, that he should go and talk to one of them instead. I was nice about it, but I said no way. And as I was telling him

that, I looked over his shoulder to where
Heladio was standing and Heladio was giving
me this look, like he was telling me he really
wanted me to talk to this guy. That about
clinched it—if Heladio told you to do
something, you did it. So I said, "Okay, I'll
talk to you, but on one condition: the only
thing I absolutely will not discuss is my
case—what I'm in for, how it went down, how
I plan to get out—none of that. And he said,

"No problem."

Okay then. So he got himself all ready and
they started filming. And the very first thing
out of his mouth was, "Steve, when you were
arrested, were you caught with marijuana?"

I was like, "Whoa! Whoa! *Cut!* Dude, what the
hell?! I just got done telling you I ain't gonna
say nothin' about my case! I haven't even
been to court yet!" (This was back when I still
thought that formalities like that mattered to
the Mexican legal system.) He apologized all
up and down and said he wouldn't ask me
things like that any more, and we started
over.

This time he didn't try asking me about my
personal situation, he just kept the focus on
the prison in general and life inside the
prison. Heladio and the comandante were
standing right there, and even though the
comandante didn't understand most of what
was being said, I knew how he'd want me to
answer. He'd want me to say everything was
great. Heladio, too: he had a good thing going,
he didn't want anybody rocking the boat. So I
was smiling away, lying through my teeth
about how they treated me well, how the food

was delicious and all that, and Johnny couldn't stop giggling about the shit I was saying, so Heladio kind of gave him the dickeye, just sort of glared at him and made him leave.

We finished with that and they stopped the camera, then Salinas told me he'd like me to take him on a little tour. He asked me where I slept, where my cell was, and I told him I lived in a little apartment called a carraca back there in the corral. He said he'd like to see it. Well, there was no way the comandante would ever go for that if he knew what we were talking about because the corral was way too dangerous. Besides, they had the shooting gallery in my tank and that would look just terrible, but Salinas was being quiet and kind of sneaky about it. Heladio and the comandante were huddled up together a little ways off, not hearing what was said. So I told Salinas, "Sure, I'll show you around."

I showed him the little square, the stores and restaurants and stuff, and it was all nice and happy. Then he went back and retraced our steps, leading the camera past everything we'd just seen while he narrated the whole thing into his microphone. I forget exactly what he said, but while he was doing this I kind of dropped back next to the cameraman, and I sort of whispered to this guy on the sly. I told him, "Last week, right where we're standing, a guy got murdered. Right here."

And he was like, "No shit?"

Yup. And I went on with it, like, "Over there are the tumbas, you know, and they got a cannibal in there..." and the guy was trying to hold the camera steady on Roberto Salinas while meanwhile he's leaning his head this way and that trying to get a peek at the stuff I'm telling him about. Up ahead the warden kept looking back, trying to make sure I was keeping it cool, and Heladio was doing the same thing. I tried to be sly about it, just trying to tell this guy the truth about the place, not that it could do any good, but it was fun and I was stoned so I didn't really care that much.

Anyway, so we went through El Pueblito, past all the little businesses and stuff, and then I led them around the corner toward the corral; I was going to try to show them my carraca. But we got just inside the gate of the corral when the warden figured out what was going on and put a stop to it. He stepped in and said something about how you can't go in the tanks because the men need their privacy or something like that. Total bullshit—he just didn't want anyone seeing how bad the conditions were in there.

That was about it. Roberto Salinas went back to San Diego and I went about my day. I guess when his report aired I was sort of the main focus of the first part of the series. Afterwards, apparently, in the intro to all the other installments there was a shot of me looking out through the fence surrounded by a bunch of vultures. I never did get to see it, but a lot of people told me about it. For a while there it seemed like everybody I ever knew or even just kind of knew back home in San Diego was watching this thing. After I got out, even, people used to come up to me all the time, everyone wanting to know me or wanting to do these big deals with me like I was some kind of Jesse James. I was just trying to get my head on straight, trying to get my health right and still having nightmares every night about that damn place, and these people were trying to get me to do crimes with them. The last thing I wanted was to jump right back into prison.

Billetera

Money From Home

I HATE TO USE THE word "celebrity," but that's kind of what I was to the friends of mine back home in the San Diego/Oceanside area who knew I was locked up down there in Mexico, especially after my TV thing aired on Channel 8. Everybody, I think, kind of liked to brag that they knew this hardened criminal, like they were somehow more legitimate or had a more interesting life because of the shit I was going through. In that scene at that time, everybody wanted to be involved in the dope business in some way or another. It was the cool thing to do. And anyway, it was just across the border, which in those days was a lot easier to deal with, so in the beginning at least I had a fair number of visitors, acquaintances and sorta-friends who'd drop by to see me and see where I was living. Not all the time, but fairly frequently. They'd stop by and we'd shoot the shit for awhile and I'd tell them stories and then I'd try to talk them out of a few bucks or a hot dog or something like that. Once in a while someone would bring me a bag of groceries, but that was rare.

So one day this buddy of mine, a good buddy named Eddie, was down visiting me and I was bitching and moaning about how people hardly ever bring me money or food, and he felt terrible about it because he had shown up empty-handed himself. I wasn't trying to make him feel bad, but he did. He said, "Shit, man, I didn't know I was allowed to bring you stuff!" And then he said, "Tell you what: I don't have nothing on me right now but I'll come back next Wednesday and I'll bring you some money so that you can buy yourself some food or dope or whatever you need. Okay?" And I said,

"Listen, Eddie, don't jerk me around here, because if I get my hopes up and you don't show, that's gonna really be a blow; that's gonna be hard to take. I mean, I would love it if you came down here and brought me something, that would really mean a lot to me, but if you say you're gonna do it you gotta make sure you really do it." He swore all up and down that he would be back the next Wednesday with some cash and a hamburger, so I said, "Great!"

Well, Wednesday rolled around and I waited and waited and of course there was no sign of Eddie; he stood me up. So I was bitter about it, of course, like "There's another disappointment." But what's one more, you know? Whatever—I let it go. Then a couple of days later I was hanging around with Johnny Bigotes, just sort of strolling around the yard. We went upstairs to this balcony area in the front of the apartments next to the basketball court, which is one of the places we sometimes hung out, and we were up there relaxing and just sort of looking around at nothing in particular. And as we were gazing out over the prison we looked to the front, to the gate area where people were coming in and out for visiting day, and we saw this crowd of vultures all bunched up around one guy in the middle. All we could see of him was his black hair and a bit of his dark skin and we just assumed he was another prisoner, because no one really messed with the visitors too much because that would have screwed things up for everybody. We figured it had to be a new guy, a new inmate. What the vultures would do is they would study the new guys coming in, to see who looked scared or confused or whatever, who had their wallet in their back pocket, you know—rookie stuff. And those are the guys they would jump on as soon as they stepped inside the gates.

We were bored as usual, so we were watching it like it was a TV show. We were like, "Oh shit, look at this, they got somebody!" We didn't really care because that's just what they did. That's what they did every day: rob someone for their stuff. To us it was something to look at, at least. So we were watching and laughing while these little vultures pushed this poor guy around, moving him along away from the front area and over toward the corral so they could rob him or beat him up or whatever they were gonna do. Then all of sudden the guy kind of turned his head as they were pushing him along, and I saw that it was Eddie. (Eddie had been born in Mexico but adopted by a white family in California, so even though he looked like he belonged there, he really didn't. He didn't know a word of Spanish, and he was sacred shitless in this situation.)

I yelled out to Johnny, I said, "Holy shit, man, that's Eddie! They got Eddie! Come on! He's got my money!" We jumped up and ran over there. I knew we didn't have much time because if they got him into the corral there was very little we'd be able to do for him. At that point we'd all be fighting for our lives; keeping hold of Eddie's wallet would be the least of our worries. So we went sprinting down there and pushed our way into the crowd. We didn't yell or punch anybody or anything like that, and we didn't even want Eddie to know we were coming for him yet because then the crowd would turn on us, too. We just waded in there like we were two more junkies out for a piece of the score.

Finally we wormed our way into the middle of the circle. I came up right behind Eddie and I could tell now that I was close to him that he was seriously freaking out. He was scared to death. His eyes were darting from side to side and he was breathing so fast I thought he was going to pass out. I got up close behind him where I could whisper in his ear and I said, "Eddie, it's me. It's Steve." I told him don't turn around, don't let on that you're hearing me. Just listen. And I told him no matter what, he had to stay with me. I said if you stay right with me I'll get you out of here. I looked down and sure enough he had his wallet in his back pocket like a dumbass, so I told him to get his hand on that wallet and keep it there, and all the while I was thinking it was a damn miracle that nobody had snagged it already because I sure would have if I were them. One of the vultures tried to make a grab for it and I slapped his hand away. He cursed me out in Spanish, but I think he knew by that point that he was in the wrong; if Eddie had been a prisoner there wasn't anything I could have done for him but because he was a visitor I was technically within my rights. The rule was: hands off the visitors.

I told Eddie we would start veering left, that we were gonna try to work our way out of that circle. And thank God, we did. With me sort of wrestling him past these vultures and Johnny coming up beside us dragging guys out of our way, we finally wriggled out until there was a little bit of daylight and then we made a break for it. We ran out of the crowd and the vultures were either too weak or too tired to run after us. They just kind of yelled at us, flipped us off a little bit, but we made it. When we got a little breathing room Eddie pulled out his wallet and forked over the fifty bucks he had for me. I thanked him for it, and then because I felt bad I bought him a hot dog with some of his own money. We hung out for a minute and then I walked him back to the gate and he left. I've seen him only once in my life after that. It was probably about fifteen years later, and he was still getting over the fear of that experience; he was only just starting to be able to see the humor in it.

¡Revolución!

Rise of the Vultures

I MENTIONED BEFORE HOW THE youngster Estrella had put himself on the map when he came through in the clutch, when even Heladio couldn't break the dry spell and somehow Estrella did it. Well, things went back to normal when Heladio's supplies picked up, I think because he had the more established organization. The bigger team, basically. Estrella couldn't take him in a head-to-head confrontation.

But the kid didn't go away entirely; he just faded into the shadows a little bit. The vultures didn't forget him, either, because Estrella was one of them. I don't know if he put the bug in their ear that Heladio was screwing them over somehow, like he was light on the weight or steep on the price or whatever, but you started to hear rumblings that the junkies were unhappy. They thought they could get a better deal if one of their own was in charge. I'm sure it got back to Heladio, and I'm sure he blew it off. Junkies are crazy; they're paranoid. The chiva was flowing, so as far as Heladio was concerned, everything was fine.

Except it wasn't. One day, I think it was almost sundown, Heladio was walking through the corral between the tanks with just two or three of his guys. I don't remember who all was with him, but one of 'em for sure was Ramón. Ramón was Heladio's number-two capo, his right-hand man in other words. He was this young, strapping cowboy type from a wealthy family in Sinaloa, I believe. They were connected to the narco trade somehow; I think they were pot farmers or maybe they grew poppies. And Ramón carried himself like that, like a rich kid who was used to getting his way. But he was tough, too. He was fierce as hell, and Heladio trusted him completely. If he didn't already, he would after this. (Ramón was also the steady boyfriend of Irma, the smoking hot blonde I first laid eyes on when she was in Heladio's bed the day Johnny Bigotes took me up there to buy a carraca. She was Ramón's girl, but every girl was Heladio's when he wanted them. That was just the way things were.)

So they were walking through the corral, talking, whatever, when one of the vultures sort of stumbled into their path. This wasn't unusual; the vultures staggered around all the time with no idea where the hell they were, they were so out of it. So one junky got right up close to Heladio, and Heladio moved like he was gonna push him aside—again, not unusual, that's just what everyone did—when all of a sudden this kid pulled out a knife and stabbed him right in the stomach!

Out of nowhere, about a dozen other vultures just swarmed on them. They all had knives or iron rebar canes. Just scrawny little strung-out dirty street junkies, and here they were mounting this coordinated attack; it was wild. I was standing right close to them, so I saw the whole thing. They piled on, stabbing and slashing and hacking away at Heladio. They got him a couple more times, bad, in his belly.

And then Ramón just went *apeshit*. It was unreal. He took his fist and I swear he just about caved this one kid's head in, just totally destroyed his face with one punch. The kid fell down like he was dead, and Ramón grabbed the knife off him, then stepped in between Heladio and the rest of them and started swinging this knife around like he was possessed. It was unbelievable how hard he fought. He must have cut at least five or six of these guys, while still punching the rest of them with his other hand and kicking them in the nuts with his cowboy boots. Eventually he grabbed a cane off one of them and he did most of the rest of his fighting with that. He was like a blur. After a few seconds of getting their asses kicked, these vultures were like, "Screw this," and they sort of fell back a bit because they were scared.

Ramón and his buddies saw that this was their big chance to get Heladio the fuck out of there because he was really in bad shape; he was all cut up, he couldn't fight at all. So they dragged him off, basically carried him, running back to his carraca. Meanwhile, the

189

vultures regrouped and ran after them, I imagine because they knew they were never gonna get another chance this good, and also they knew that if they didn't finish him off, Heladio would come back for revenge and then they'd be fucked. So they chased after him, and I and everybody else who was rubbernecking this whole deal chased after them, because this was major—this was the biggest thing to ever happen in there as far as we were concerned.

We all went running out of the corral over to the square, and the vultures ran up the stairs to Heladio's carraca, but they couldn't get in because Heladio's guys had the steel security door shut tight. The vultures were yelling and banging on the screen, but it was no use, they couldn't get in. So they dispersed, we all did, because by now the guards were coming and we knew they'd be in a shooting mood after all this shit. So everybody scattered.

The guards ran up the stairs and talked to Ramón through the gate for a little while. Then they brought over a stretcher from the infirmary, and a little while later there was an armed escort, with the guards all circled around Heladio's guys as they carried him out on the stretcher. They were taking him to the hospital because there was no way in hell he was going to make it without a real hospital working on him. I just caught a glimpse of him, and I was like,

"Holy shit. Heladio's dying."

Sueño

Blind Murder

I'M NOT SURE IF THIS next story is directly related to the power struggle between Heladio and Estrella, but it happened around that same time and it just goes to show how crazy and on-edge everyone felt.

What happened was, the head capo in my tank, this guy Mundo, was married to the sister of Flaco, who was another guy in the tank. Mundo and his wife used to love to sit in their carraca at night and eat their Mandrax. They did it almost every night, every chance they got. And so one night they were getting high eating the Mandrax, and Mundo got paranoid. Then he turned violent; he beat her up real bad. She ran out—she was screaming and crying and stuff—and she ran down to her brother's carraca so he could protect her. Flaco up until this point had been good friends with Mundo; they were tight. But when he saw his sister all beat up he went to Mundo's room to confront him, and he ended up stabbing Mundo a bunch of times. He didn't kill him, but he stabbed him repeatedly. The tank capo!

So Mundo went to the hospital for a while, but he couldn't afford to stay there until he was fully recovered. The way it worked was you had to pay your own way if you were going to get actual hospital care. Mundo could only afford the most basic emergency care necessary to save his life and stitch him up. He was only in the hospital a day or two before they brought him back to the tank to continue his recovery. They hauled him up to his carraca and laid him out on his bed. Now, in the meantime, while he was still in the hospital, he had sent word back to Flaco that there wasn't going to be any retribution, that he wouldn't hold it against him, because Flaco was just sticking up for his sister. It was water under the bridge. Mundo was saying he deserved it, basically, but it's possible he was simply trying to make sure Flaco didn't come after him again, because he knew he was going to be in a weakened state when he came back into the tank.

Anyway, where I say this incident sort of reflects the general paranoia going around at the time is that Flaco didn't buy it. Mundo promised him everything was forgiven and he refused to believe it. He went out and bought a pistol, a nine millimeter, because he was totally convinced it was a trick, that Mundo was setting him up. He decided he wasn't gonna wait around for Mundo to get revenge on him; he was gonna attack him first. And because they were friends before this and Flaco had been in Mundo's carraca dozens of times to hang out, he knew where everything was, how it was all laid out. For instance, he knew, that Mundo's bed was right along the front wall next to the door, and that Mundo always slept with his head to the right, and he knew how high the bed was.

So one night Flaco went creeping right up to the wall outside Mundo's carraca. He lined up the pistol and emptied it into the wall. Remember, these walls were basically cardboard, they didn't even count when it came to stopping a bullet. This guy pumped all these shots into the wall and every single one of them hit Mundo where he was sleeping on the other side. BOOM BOOM BOOM BOOM! In his head, in his chest, in his stomach. Killed him right there, multiple times over. I don't know what happened to Flaco after that. I don't even know if his sister appreciated it.

Cojo

Careful What You Wish For

WHEN HELADIO WAS STABBED, EVERYTHING went crazy. They locked everybody down, suspended visiting privileges, the whole deal. They wanted to make sure we weren't going to burn the place down or anything. But as long as the drugs kept flowing and there weren't any more open gunfights in the yard, the average prisoner could care less. In the confusion, the youngster Estrella stepped up to take charge of the heroin market, and that kept things under control for the most part. It was a real uneasy calm, though, as you can probably imagine.

I would have thought that Ramón, Heladio's number two, would have stepped into the head capo role. But he did a smart thing: as soon as they let us back out to circulate again, he went to consult with The Brothers. Robert and Johnny were huge on the streets of L.A.; to them, figuring out the politics inside our little city was nothing. It was like tee ball to them. They'd know what to do.

I happened to be hanging out playing cards with Johnny when Ramón showed up. He came in looking pretty shellshocked and said he wanted to get Johnny's take on the situation. They asked me to split while they talked, which I was happy to do because there's a lot of things you're just better off not knowing, but before I left they both told me not to worry, that everything would be back to normal soon. I took that to mean that they were going to knock off Estrella, that they were just biding their time for now.

What I gathered from talking to them later— just bits and pieces here and there—was that they were going to wait and see. Estrella was such a dipshit that I think they half expected him to flame out on his own before they had to do anything about him. Either way, nothing had been done that couldn't be undone; Ramón had the experience and the manpower to take over whenever he wanted and everybody knew it except Estrella and his raggedy-ass gang of vultures. They were real cocky for a while there. They thought they were untouchable now that they were in the driver's seat.

In all of this, the thing no one said, I think because they didn't have to, was that they were waiting to see if Heladio would live or die. We were getting daily reports through the grapevine back from the hospital. He had suffered a lot of internal damage, and they were still worried about infection. He was conscious but very weak, and they still didn't know for sure if he'd be able to return to La Mesa or if they'd have to keep him in the prison ward of the hospital for the rest of his sentence. That would have a major impact on Ramón's options, whether Heladio was in the picture or not. Even though Ramón was respected and well-liked, Heladio was the kingpin. If he did come back, with a big triumphant return, the whole crew could ride the momentum of that right back into power. If he didn't, Ramón would have a much tougher time. Best to wait for now and play it cool. So that's what he did.

As the days went on, it became fairly clear that Heladio was gonna be okay, and that made it a lot easier for Ramón to bide his time. He just kicked back with a little smile on his face and watched it all play out. The vultures saw Estrella as their *campeón*, their champion, and he let it all go to his head almost as soon as he established himself as head capo. He was always kind of a cocky prick, but now he was just ridiculous. He started carrying a little black book, like a small ledger, around with him everywhere he went, and he used it to keep track of everyone who owed him money (or everyone he said owed him money). But he kept the heroin flowing, so the vultures took it. However, I think they pretty quickly regretted putting their weight behind that guy.

Estrella's biggest weakness, though, was he simply didn't know what the hell he was doing. He didn't have the brains or the temperament or the experience to head up a big organization. Heladio, by comparison, always made sure his guys knew who was boss, but he also made sure to treat them like junior partners. He'd give them little bonuses here and there, hand out papers of chiva or pot at the end of meetings, that kind of thing. He'd make sure the hookers took care of them. And they'd give their lives for him. Compared to that, Estrella was dumber than shit. He didn't do any of that, and his organization came off as being exactly what it was: a bunch of confused junkies pretending to be a gang.

So anyway, it was two or three weeks after the stabbing, and Heladio was almost well enough to come back. I'm not sure if it came down from him or Ramón or somebody else, but it was apparently decided that it would be best if Estrella wasn't around when Heladio made his return; it'd be better if he were dead. So the job went to this young street kid who was always hanging around Heladio's guys, always trying to get his foot in the door of their organization. He hadn't been in long, but as soon as he got there, he figured out which crew was the best and just pursued them like a dog with a bone. So I guess his tenacity impressed them. This kid— Alejandro was his name—was skinny and dirty like everybody else, and he got around on this shaky homemade crutch because I guess he'd been shot before they brought him in. I don't know if the cops shot him or somebody else did, but he had a bad leg and he would limp around on this crutch of his. He was a pretty pathetic figure when you got right down to it, but he was also just an evil, soulless little piece of shit. I think in the end that was his main qualification.

But he couldn't do it all by himself. True, he didn't look like a threat, but the vulture who took down Heladio didn't, either. Even as naïve and cocky as Estrella was, the element of surprise was pretty much played out; no one would fall for that again anytime soon. For the hit to work, they needed a distraction. As it turned out, Alejandro had a buddy in Estrella's crew. They knew each other from the streets. Gordo was his name, which means "fat," and he was. For a little bit of cash, Gordo agreed to help set up Estrella.

They planned to do it on the soccer field. That's where Estrella was always at his cockiest, and where they figured he'd be most likely to be thinking about himself and not about whether or not someone had plans to off him. There was a prison team—I forget what they were called, the Tigers or something—and Estrella was like the captain of the team. They would play against teams from outside. All home games, obviously; the Tigers didn't travel. Anyway, so this happened on a day when another team had come in to play against the prison team, and there was a big crowd of visitors, including Estrella's wife and kids. His wife was real pretty and he had two kids, a boy and a girl, about three or four years old. They were standing on the sidelines watching the game.

So halftime rolled around and Estrella came over to the side to get a drink, and that's when Gordo called him over to give him a little sniff of coke, a little bump. Gordo held up the spoon for Estrella, and right as he was snorting this coke, Alejandro came limping out of the crowd behind him with a pistol in his hand. He shot him right in the middle of the back. Gordo backed up as Estrella crumpled to the ground, and everybody scattered from the sound of the gun, but they were also craning their necks, whipping their heads all around trying to see who had been shot. As Estrella was groaning and trying to crawl away, Alejandro limped up behind him and put a second shot right in the back of his head. That was it. As soon as it was done, he dropped the gun and put his hands up, just waiting for the guards to come and grab him. Immediately, at the first shot, Estrella's wife started freaking out, just screaming uncontrollably. The guards ran up; some of them hustled her and her kids out toward the gate, others grabbed Alejandro and dragged him off in the same direction. That's the last we'll see of that kid, I figured.

Estrella's body was still lying there, facedown in the dirt. All of a sudden his guys pounced on it, all of them at once like a feeding frenzy. They grabbed everything of value: his chains, his shoes, his watch. They picked him clean. His number-two capo, this real treacherous older guy named Diablo, snagged what he figured was the most valuable thing of all: Estrella's little black ledger book.

Rey

The Return of Heladio

A SHORT TIME LATER, HELADIO came back. ~~Jesus Christ~~, was that ever a scene! It seemed as if the entire prison population had turned out to see him. There were literally hundreds of people crowding around the main entrance. Guards, prisoners, families, everybody. If you had been planning an escape attempt, that would have been the time to do it, as long as you were going out on the other side, away from the gate. It was a ghost town over there.

Anyway, even though he wasn't totally better just yet, it was important to Heladio to return under his own steam. He had to walk in with his head up high so everybody could see he wasn't afraid. They'd tried to kill him, but here he was, still the top dog, you know? And it's true, he *was* the top dog, more popular than ever. In some ways that attempt on his

201

life was the thing that made him a legend. He was well-known before that, but afterward he was much more famous. Nowadays it's common to have songs written to glorify drug lords, killers, etc., but in those days I think it was still kind of a novelty. There was a new one playing on the radio as he walked in; they must have planned it, because every radio around was tuned to the same station and at that exact moment when he was limping into the prison, they were playing a song about how Heladio Diaz was unkillable, a total gangster superstar. It was a trip.

He came in all alone, which was symbolic in a way, too, because it really showed he wasn't afraid, and even though you could tell he was hurting more than he let on, he smiled and waved to everybody as he walked slowly across the yard to his carraca. A couple of his capos were there to help him up the stairs and then he went inside and pretty much stayed there for a couple more weeks until he was fully recovered. I think he maybe jumped the gun a little bit coming back so soon, but with Estrella gone he wanted to reassert himself before anyone else tried to fill the void.

Even with Heladio back in La Mesa, with everything supposedly back to normal, there was still a lot of tension around at that time. Starting with the stabbing of Heladio, then with the murder of Estrella, it really felt like shit was spinning out of control. We all wondered if anyone was crazy enough to take another shot at Heladio, and the vultures were shitting themselves with fear that Heladio was gonna come after them for retribution, even as they kept buying his chiva. Estrella's little organization had mostly disbanded, but everyone knew who they were, and that must have driven those guys crazy, the fear of what was gonna happen to them. They started turning on each other, they were so freaked out.

First they went after Gordo, the fat-ass who set up Estrella that day on the field. Even if the kid Alejandro, the one who'd actually pulled the trigger, hadn't disappeared to who-knows-where, they couldn't have made a move on him anyway because he was with Heladio now. He was too well connected; no one wanted to fuck with that. But Gordo was a nobody, a traitor with no friends. He was fair game. I happened to be right there when it went down. It was evening lockdown, when everyone had to go back to the tanks for the night. I was sort of dragging my ass, slow-walking along; there were only about four or five of us total out there. I was almost to the corral when all of a sudden I heard some yelling coming from behind me in the yard. I turned and saw that it was Gordo and these other guys, two or three other guys who were also part of Estrella's crew. They were yelling at Gordo, calling him out, calling him names.

The reason they were so pissed is they couldn't believe how fast everything had gotten fucked up. One minute they're part of the dominant gang, they're on top of the world, and the next minute they're running around with targets on their backs, freaking out because they're gonna get killed now. That's what their thinking was, anyway, and I don't think they were wrong. And they blamed it all on Gordo because he had ruined everything for the price of a few bucks.

So anyway, these guys were yelling at Gordo and he was trying to back away from them, but they got him cornered and then he tried begging, which is just not something you do, so that pissed them off even worse. They each had one of those rebar canes that everybody favored, three feet of iron rebar bent up at one end like a walking cane and wrapped around and around with melted plastic from pop bottles, like Bubble-Up bottles or whatever. They would wrap that hot plastic around the rebar and then let it cool to make a covering on it. They'd make patterns with the different colors; some of them were really elaborate. I'm not sure if the plastic was for grip, or just to look cool, or maybe just so it wasn't quite so obvious that you were walking around with a metal rod to smack people with. But these guys had them and they started hitting Gordo with them, hard. Gordo went down and they just keep whaling on him with the rebar. And the thing I'll never forget is the *sound* that fucking guy made. Here was this great big fat guy, first of all, and then when they started really going to work on him he began literally squealing like a pig. It was horrible to listen to him. I mean, you could say he deserved it, but it was horrible. It was horrible to hear it.

That bloodcurdling squeal is probably what saved his life, though, because a guard came running, and he started firing his gun into the ground until the guys hitting him just broke and ran, leaving Gordo writhing in the dirt, still making that sound. It took him a few seconds to realize they weren't whipping him anymore. Then he picked himself up, slowly because they'd got him real good, and he started limping back to the corral, back to wherever he slept. He wasn't squealing anymore, but he was still sort of crying, like softly weeping, which in some ways was even worse.

That was a weird scene, a sad scene. That one's stuck with me.

Diablo

Heladio Meets the Devil

AFTER THE KID ALEJANDRO SHOT Estrella down, then shot him again, the guards dragged him off and we all thought—or at least I did, anyway—that he was a goner. I thought they'd take him away and kill him, chop up his body and throw it in the dump. (That's what the rumor always was whenever there was an unexplained disappearance; we thought whoever it was was put in the dump.) But that wasn't the case this time. After about two weeks, Alejandro came back, looking like a million bucks.

Before he left, he was this mangy, scrawny, dirty little junky-looking guy with his raggedy, bloody clothes and his shitty homemade crutch. Now he was all cleaned up and fed, with a good haircut and real nice clothes. He had brand new everything: expensive boots, a nice leather jacket, the whole bit. He was still limping from when he had been shot in the leg before, but now instead of his rickety crutch he had a new shiny cane with a silver tip on it. He looked like a total big shot, and you knew right away that Heladio had hooked him up. He was part of that crew now, and he carried himself like a made man. Which I guess he was.

Heladio was fully in charge again by this point, holding court on his balcony overlooking the square. He was selling more chiva than ever, and still getting his cut of everything that went on. Johnny Brother was right—it was just a matter of waiting for all the craziness to blow over. Heladio was even back to sponsoring fiestas. Overall, it was a nice, calm, stable time for everybody. No one seemed to miss Estrella, who had always been a dick anyway, and no one seemed interested in making a move against Heladio. So we all breathed easy.

In La Mesa, any time things seemed good, it wouldn't last for long. Prison will punish your optimism every time. So we should have known something bad was coming down. Even if we'd expected it, though, we couldn't have known what form it would take.

In general, the way killings and other attacks worked is they were pretty much always business. Occasionally there'd be a crime of passion like that crazy situation with Mundo and the other guy's sister, but those were rare. For the most part there had to be money in it. After Estrella was murdered, there was no incentive for anyone to go after Heladio, because no one was paying them to do it. No one wanted it that bad. In my experience, killings over revenge or honor don't happen that often; it's just not worth it.

But the thing that no one anticipated was how bad Estrella's family on the outside missed him. I can't imagine why, but they must have really loved that guy, because they came up with the money to put a hit on Heladio for no reason but straight-up vengeance. And killing a guy like Heladio doesn't come cheap. Even though there were a lot of desperate people around, a lot of desperate murderers, this is still probably at least a thousand dollars we're talking about.

The guy they hired for the job was Diablo, Estrella's second capo. He was older, over thirty I would guess, but he looked older than that. He wore a red bandana, he had long hair, he was just a real treacherous guy, as you might expect from the name. After Estrella's death, in that brief period before Heladio came back to reclaim the throne or whatever, Diablo had gone around with Estrella's little black ledger book and tried to collect on all the debts that people owed Estrella. When Heladio came back, he pretty much laid low.

Anyway, in the old days Heladio would usually be surrounded by bodyguards whenever he walked through the yard. Not always, but he had a security presence around him fairly regularly. After they stabbed him, though, he stepped it up; you *never* saw him without his bodyguards after the stabbing—except on this one particular day when he went out by himself. They let him leave the prison for some reason or other, to see his lawyer or visit a woman or something like that. And he must have come back at a different time than he'd planned to, because when he came back his guys weren't there to meet him; he had to cross the prison by himself back to his carraca.

I think now, in hindsight, that Diablo must have had something to do with the change in Heladio's schedule. How else to explain it? Diablo was pretty treacherous, as I said, so I think he could have engineered it. Maybe he called whoever Heladio was supposed to see and cancelled the meeting or something. Either way, by luck or by design, he was camped out waiting when Heladio came back by himself. When he saw that Heladio was alone, he set up in this sort of corridor area between a couple of tanks, knowing he'd have to pass by there. He was leaning on the wall when Heladio walked by. I happened to be there too, not in the corridor, but out in the corral. I was pretty far away but I had a clear view.

I saw them sort of nod at each other, like they were saying hello. Not friendly, just a show of respect. As Heladio passed, Diablo pulled a gun out from the back of his pants, from his waistband back there under his shirt. He shot Heladio right in the middle of the back, and the bullet went clear through him; you could see daylight out the other side. Heladio just toppled forward and was dead before he hit the ground. Just like that.

This time, the guards were all over it. I don't know if they'd seen it or what, but somehow they and the federales just came swooping in from everywhere all at once. They herded everyone out of there with bursts from their big-ass machine guns, the way they did when it was really serious. The death of Heladio Diaz was about as serious as you could get in that place; it would be the same thing as someone assassinating the president. So they chased all of us off the yard and back to our carracas for lockdown—they locked the whole prison down—and just before I went around the corner and lost sight of Heladio lying there, I saw something that I will never forget. One of the guards was kneeling down next to Heladio's body, and he rolled him over, like he wanted to make sure he was really dead. Now Heladio was lying there on his back with this hole in his chest—blood everywhere, he was covered with it—and this guard took his pointer finger, one finger, and he just, like, poked it into the hole in Heladio's chest. Just poked it in there all the way to the hilt. Then he pulled it back out slowly and looked at it, staring at the blood on his finger as it ran down his hand.

Then they pushed me and the other guys and we had to move on, but that image has stuck with me to this day, and I'm sure it'll stick with me forever, because why would you do that? Why would anybody want to stick their finger in a guy's chest like that? I can't figure it out. Was he trying to feel his heart? Did he just want to be able to say, I felt Heladio's heart? What would make you do something like that?

Anyway, in the chaos that immediately followed, Diablo got dragged out just like Alejandro had after he killed Estrella. They took him to La Ocho, I think, to keep him safe from Heladio's guys. And after a while Diablo came back, just like Alejandro, but he wasn't all slicked-up like the kid had been. He wasn't a big shot now. If anything he seemed smaller. No one made a move to get back at him—I think everyone just wanted it to be over with.

With Heladio out of the picture, there was a real brief freakout, but only because guys were afraid that the taste, the chiva, would be cut off. Sure, it was unsettling to think that even someone as powerful as Heladio could be taken out, but that was minor in the big scheme of things; it's not like any of us really felt safe before that, so we weren't that much more afraid afterwards. And you might expect there to be some kind of emotional response after such a major player is suddenly out of the picture, but that just wasn't the case. Maybe there was a big funeral out on the street, with everybody crying and laying flowers on his grave and all that, but inside it was just another day. That's the truth of it.

The guy they put in charge—and by "they" I mean The Brothers and another big criminal family who I'd rather not name—was a lower-ranking capo in Heladio's organization. He would have been maybe about the number-four or number-five guy on the totem pole, not real impressive, but someone they could trust to take orders and not get any big ideas. As for Ramón, who I would have figured to be the obvious choice to take over, he pretty much kept right on doing what he'd always done: he'd sell his heroin and lay low in his carraca with his girlfriend Irma until his wife and kids came to visit. Then he'd kick Irma out until the coast was clear and then she'd be back. He didn't really play much of a political role in La Mesa after Heladio was gone. I think he preferred it that way. Heladio's other girl, Elsa, left the prison and didn't come back, and as for the boy Bobby, he was already long gone by this point. He wasn't a prisoner, so he had left earlier, I think around the time of Heladio's stabbing, when things turned really tense inside. But this all went down fairly soon before I got out, so I can't say for certain if there were any longer-term ripples that resulted from the killing of Heladio. From where I was sitting, it sure seemed like it was just business as usual from one day to the next, as unlikely as it sounds now.

Dragón

The Lady
and the Dragon

I'VE NEVER BEEN A RELIGIOUS person by any stretch of the imagination, not even superstitious, but something happened shortly before my release that made me wonder whether things are maybe a little bit more connected than they seem at first glance.

In those days, at the time I was there, La Mesa didn't have a big missionary presence. You didn't see as many nuns or Catholic relief workers as you did in later years. I'm not sure why exactly, but that's the way it was. There was just one main lady who used to come in and talk to us, try to save our souls or whatever. She was very nice, and easy to talk to, but I let her know right off the bat that I wasn't interested in the whole Jesus thing she was pushing. She didn't care, she still liked to talk to me, so we would talk for a while whenever she came in to visit.

One day she said she wanted to see where I lived, to check out the conditions. I took her into the tank and we climbed up to my carraca. To her credit, she didn't seem scared at all even though the inside of the tanks was always a pretty freaky scene. So we were in my carraca, making small talk, when she noticed this print I had on my wall. I had an artist buddy back home who was pretty big in the underground rock scene, doing concert posters and stuff like that, and he had given me this framed print of one of his pictures. He was a good friend of mine but he was a really trippy dude, very much into freaky, mystical, far-out stuff, and that came out in his art. This picture was pretty wild: it had a big bare-breasted warrior woman as its main thing—I think she had a sword or an axe or something; huge tits, definitely—and she was sort of rubbing up on this big dragon. It was a really cool picture, and I would conservatively estimate that I had jerked off to it probably over five hundred times, so I felt like a creep standing there with this nice religious lady looking at it.

She told me I had to get rid of the dragon-lady picture, that I was putting my soul in danger just by having it in my place. She said that until I took that picture down and burned it I would never get out of La Mesa. Whatever. I said I'd think about it, and she went on her way. A couple weeks later she came back and I saw her out in the yard. She asked me if I'd dealt with the evil picture yet. I told her I hadn't, but in the couple weeks that had passed since she talked to me about it, I'd begun to get a bad feeling from it. It was like she'd gotten into my head and ruined it for me. So I told her she could have it. We went back up to my place and I took it off the wall and gave it to her. She covered it with a cloth right away, as if it was dangerous to leave it exposed. She told me I was doing the right thing.

A short while later she sent word that she'd had a little ceremony where she said some prayers and burned the picture. It was done, she said; good things would happen for me now. And right after that, I found out I was being released. So trip out on that.

Llave

Going Home

THE MEXICAN LEGAL SYSTEM IS
notoriously corrupt, and in those days, I
believe, it was even worse than it is
now. Everything was disorganized and
informal and handled under the table or
behind closed doors. In the vast majority of
cases, your chances to beat the charges or to
get off with a light sentence had very little to
do with your guilt or innocence, or the
seriousness of the crime, but by your ability
to buy your way out of it.

In a smuggling case like mine, the first step
was to try to get the sentence reduced to
under five years. (Obviously, the real first
step would be to try to beat the rap entirely,
but that wasn't an option for me because in
signing the declaration that let Roger and
Barbara go, I'd basically pleaded guilty.) If
you were sentenced to five years or more, you
had to do the time; there was no getting
around it. If, on the other hand, you somehow
managed to keep your sentence to under five
years, suddenly a whole new set of options

opened up to you. Under five years, there was hope.

What put me in a good position with respect to finding a lawyer was the fact that I'd kept my mouth shut. At no point did I even hint that I might be willing to roll over on my connection. Understand, I definitely could have. I could have given up Mexico Joe who'd supplied us the pot as well as everyone else a step or two up the ladder from him. But I would never do that because I think it's wrong and, besides, it's stupid. Keeping your mouth shut goes a long way towards earning respect in any prison. Nobody likes a snitch, and people will treat you nicer if they know you have a sense of honor and you take that seriously. So in my case, powerful people were happy to hook me up with a first-rate attorney because they liked that I kept my mouth shut.

Everyone told me the same thing: that the man to see was Rudolfo Lopez. He was the biggest lawyer in Tijuana at the time, and he was always helping guys in the drug business win their cases or reduce their sentences. He had a great track record, so when word came back that he was willing to talk to me, I was beyond happy. We finally met up when he came to La Mesa to see another client. After their meeting, he hung around for a few minutes to listen to the details of my case. I met him out near the gate. He was an imposing guy, probably in his mid-forties I would guess, and dressed real sharp in a nice suit and expensive-looking shoes. He looked like what he was—a successful lawyer.

I explained to him what I knew about my case, which wasn't much, frankly. I knew I'd been picked up by the city cops, who'd then turned me over to the federales who were the ones that eventually charged me. I hadn't been sentenced as far as I knew, and I didn't have the foggiest idea where my case stood now. Not a lot of information there. He didn't seem too worried; he said he knew everyone there was to know in the whole court system and that he'd get to the bottom of it and let me know what he learned. In the meantime, he told me, my job was to start raising money: for expenses, for bribes, and—most importantly—for his fee.

I scraped up what little I had, then put the word out to basically everyone I'd ever met that I needed cash in a hurry to get myself out of prison. I think I was able to come up with several hundred dollars, which I handed over to Lopez the next time he came to La Mesa. He explained to me that my case was in the hands of the local judge, whose job it was to determine my sentence. If he gave me five years or more, I was screwed, but if he kept it under five years then I'd likely be eligible for *fianza,* or bail. If I could get out on bail while appealing my case, that could make all the difference in the world to my health and sanity (not that that was the plan, exactly, but more on that in a minute). He said he thought he could keep my sentence under five years for a few hundred bucks. I gave him all I had. He told me to keep scrounging money; we were nowhere near finished yet.

A few weeks later he came back and told me the local judge had entered a sentence of four years, six months. That was a long time, obviously, but a lot better than it could have been. At least the hope of bail was still there. The next step was for the sentence to go up the chain to the federal court in Hermosillo, where it would be reviewed by another judge who had the authority either to rubber-stamp it or throw it out and enter his own sentence. Of course, the federal judge would expect a few dollars for his trouble. I made my calls, raised the money, and the sentence was approved.

The way fianza worked, it was essentially a cross between bail and parole. You were still subject to the sentence, meaning they could revoke your bail whenever they wanted and throw you back in prison to serve out your time, but in the meantime you were free to leave while you waited and worked on your appeal. You just had to check in with an officer every Saturday. (That way they made sure that if you did run, you never had more than a week-long head start, I guess; I'm not really sure about the logic of that.)

Anyway, Rudolfo Lopez sent word that my fianza had been approved—all I had to do was come up with the bail amount and his fee, a total of $6400. More than almost anything else in this whole ordeal, that dollar figure felt like a punch in the gut. How in the hell was I supposed to come up with $6400?! Well, with no other option but to try, I got back on the phone; I took up a collection around the prison; I reached out to everyone I'd ever met—again—and most of all, I put the screws to Roger. I had just spent almost a year of my life in the worst prison in Mexico for a crime he'd committed as well, so I'd be ~~goddamned~~ if I was gonna let him get away without paying his fair share (which, as far as I was concerned, was all of it). It took some time and some convincing, but Roger came through in the end. I will always be grateful to him for that.

It seemed like everyone else in La Mesa knew I'd made bail before I did; I remember Johnny Bigotes came down to wherever I was—the hot dog stand, probably—with all of my stuff in a box. He'd packed up my whole carraca, everything I could possibly want, and he handed it to me. He said, "You're going home, Steve. You're getting out."

I thought he was messing with me; I didn't believe it. I think I had spent so much time and energy getting my mind to a place where I could deal with being locked up that I just couldn't make the transition to seeing myself as a free man. I was in shock. But he pressed this box into my hands and walked me to the front gate and pushed me towards it. I remember there were other guys there, too, The Brothers and Ramón and a bunch of the transvestites and other inmates, and they were all waving at me and saying goodbye. It didn't feel real. I just floated on that feeling all the way out through the gate until they locked it behind me, and then I just broke down. I didn't want them to see me crying, but it was just so confusing and such a relief and scary at the same time. It was just too much.

The plan all along was to do what everybody did in those days: make bail and skip bail. For Americans locked up in Mexico, fianza was almost as good as a full pardon. Once you

walked out through those gates, you could
stroll right across the border and be home in
the States. You just couldn't go back to
Mexico, not if you wanted to be safe. I pushed
my luck for a few weeks, checking in on
Saturdays like I was supposed to while I
came back to visit and bring food, money and
girls to my buddies still inside. I was also
working to help Johnny Bigotes get released,
which we were eventually able to do when
Davy came up with the money. It didn't take
long, though, before I became simply too
freaked out to go back. I knew they could
change their minds at any time and hold me
for the rest of my sentence. That weighed on
my mind, so when I couldn't take it any more,
I went north across the border for the last
time and never looked back.

It's more than 35 years later now and I'm still
standing, which is more than I can say for El
Pueblito. Before dawn on August 20th, 2002,
guards stormed through the prison in a last-
ditch effort to get La Mesa under control.
They rounded up more than a thousand
inmates, driving them out of their carracas
and the little businesses they ran and lived
in, and took them away to other prisons and
other parts of La Mesa. Then the bulldozers
came in. For a whole day they rolled through,
destroying everything the prisoners had
created, erasing all traces of what had made
La Mesa special. They even kicked out the
kids and the wives and the parents. It was the
end of an era.

As the years went by, the entire country of
Mexico came to resemble more and more
what La Mesa had been at its peak: a wild,

lawless place, enslaved by drugs and ruled by the whims of the *narcos* at the top of the food chain. As for La Mesa itself, it became just a typical prison with typical prison problems. The last straw came in 2008, when a young prisoner was beaten to death by the guards, setting off two massive riots in the span of three days. Hundreds were injured in the violence that followed, and dozens of inmates lost their lives.

I still think about La Mesa almost every day. I remember the scary times and the good times, the friends I made and the terrible things I saw. It was years before I could sleep through the night without waking up screaming from awful nightmares of the walls closing in on me, crushing me in a little box. But even with all that, I can't say I look back on that year with regret. Not entirely. It was a challenge, no question, but I got to experience a world that most people can never imagine, and I survived it. In that sense, I feel fortunate; not many people can say that.

And if nothing else, I came away with some pretty cool stories to tell.

The day I got out. Compare this picture to the one they shot when they first brought us in. Roger looks the same; I look about twenty years older.

That's what my time in La Mesa did to me.

ABOUT THE AUTHORS

Growing up, STEVE PETERSON dreamed of becoming a cowboy, a sailor, a fisherman and a smuggler. All of these dreams came true, and then some.

His greatest joy is being a father of six, with six grandkids and counting...

•••••••

ELDON ASP is a writer of various scripts and stories, mostly involving characters who are very excited about their horrible plans. LOCKED UP IN LA MESA is his first book.

His next one is EASY STREET.

10951640R0

Made in the USA
Lexington, KY
03 September 2011